LAWNS

Mr Escritt has for many years been Director of the Sports Turf Research Institute in Yorkshire, the recognised national centre on amenity turf of all kinds. He has travelled extensively in connection with the Institute's Research and Advisory work and has visited many parts of Europe, Canada, the USA, Mexico, Africa, the Middle East, Australia and New Zealand.

Mr Escritt has from time to time contributed popular articles on lawns to various magazines and periodicals. He co-authored the book *Sports Ground Construction – Specifications* with Mr R. B. Gooch of the National Playing Fields Association (published by the NPFA) and has recently written a comprehensive book on amenity turf *ABC of Turf Culture* (Kaye & Ward Ltd.).

TEACH YOURSELF BOOKS

The World of the Garden

Series editor: Professor Alan Gemmell

The Basics of Gardening Alan Gemmell
Lawns J. R. Escritt
Growing Vegetables Tony Briggs

To be published

Garden Flowers S. B. Whitehead
Growing Fruit R. Genders
Trees and Shrubs P. Hemsley
Greenhouses C. Hart

LAWNS

J. R. Escritt, M.Sc.

Series Editor:
Professor Alan Gemmell

Illustrations by:
Oriol Bath

with the author's compliment

J Escritt

7.2.84

TEACH YOURSELF BOOKS
Hodder and Stoughton

ISBN 0 340 23479 2

Printed and bound in Great Britain for
Hodder and Stoughton Paperbacks, a division of Hodder and
Stoughton Ltd, Mill Road, Dunton Green, Sevenoaks, Kent,
(Editorial Office: 47 Bedford Square, London WC1 3DP)
by Richard Clay (The Chaucer Press) Ltd,
Bungay, Suffolk

Published in the U.S.A. by David McKay & Co. Inc.,
750 Third Avenue, New York, N.Y. 10017, U.S.A.

Contents

List of Illustrations

Introduction

The British home lawn is the envy of the world and it is only when one sees the attempts of some other nations to copy it that one realises that the average British gardener is remarkably successful in lawn construction and maintenance. There is no doubt that nature helps a great deal—the temperate climate favours the growth of a few species of grass which tolerate regular mowing and are therefore suitable for lawns. Furthermore, in temperate zones there are not the extremes of heat, cold, dryness or wetness experienced in some parts of the world and this is also an advantage. Moreover, the numbers and kinds of weeds, pests and diseases which occur are decidedly limited. Hence, there are few real problems for prospective owners of good lawns in the United Kingdom provided that they observe a few simple rules. The same is true, of course, for those other parts of the world which have a temperate climate. I have seen for myself some very good lawns (comparable with Britain's best) in similar climatic conditions, in North America and, of course, in New Zealand.

Lawn troubles usually result from neglect (through lack of appreciation of the need for a little *regular* attention) or from trying too hard (especially in trying to implement *all* the advice offered so freely by so many self-styled experts). This book sets out to help everyone who wants to produce and maintain a decent lawn, whether it be as small as a billiard table or as large as a hockey pitch.

The definition of what constitutes a 'decent lawn' is entirely up to the owner! The main values of any kind of area of mown grass to the home and garden lover are the pleasing impression the lawn gives when the house is approached, the pleasant view it offers from the windows and the way it sets off the flower beds. While the connoisseur may wish to have a lawn which is mainly to look at and preferably resembles a bowling green or golf green, many people require their lawn to perform a variety of duties—to function as a playground for the children, to provide space for clothes drying outdoors and/or to furnish pleasant surrounds for simply sitting in the sun and fresh air, or for having outdoor tea-parties! The kind of turf to have is the one that best reconciles the owner's requirements with the time and effort which can be put into producing and maintaining it.

To help in the understanding of the practical guidance given in the rest of the book, the first chapter gives basic information on just how a lawn area is made up. The first section of this chapter deals with the actual grass, the second with the soil below it and the third with drainage of the soil with practical guidance on coping with wet sites. Drainage in all its aspects is of the utmost consequence for bowling greens and for all sports turf areas but the need for pipe drainage on lawns seems to arise comparatively rarely. Nevertheless a desire for guidance is frequently encountered and real problems do occur from time to time.

Although there are many more people concerned with looking after an existing lawn than there are engaged in creating a new lawn it seemed logical to put lawn making at the beginning of the book, especially as, if a lawn is not well made in the first place, it is the more likely that some of the troubles described later in the book will occur.

Next comes the section on routine management of existing lawns with the accent very much on what is almost the only essential requirement, i.e. mowing. (Brief sections at the end of the book detail maintenance equipment and seasonal work.)

The chapter on lawn troubles is by far the longest in the book since it attempts to answer as many as possible of lawn owners' questions on large and small problems. It is hoped that the production of such a long list is not found frightening. Just as there are many millions of healthy people in the world despite the catalogue of woes in a home-doctor book, so there must be countless lawns without any of the problems described, many of which are in any case very minor and easily dealt with. In the ordinary way it is really not very difficult at all to maintain a lawn—all it needs is a *little* but *regular* attention which should in itself give pleasure and satisfaction.

Finally a brief glossary explains some of the terms which may be unfamiliar to the non-technical reader; a list of books for further reading is also provided.

A word about safety precautions should not come amiss though broadly they can all be described as using common sense. Unfortunately common sense is not as common as we would like it to be and there is a tendency for familiarity to breed contempt. Mowers can be very dangerous if used carelessly and certainly no adjustments or repairs should be carried out unless they are immobilised, for example, by disconnecting sparking plugs.

Gardeners in general, including lawn owners, may find it necessary from time to time to use toxic chemical preparations. The greatest possible care should be taken in storage and use of chemicals, especially where there are children or pets around (whether the user's or the neighbour's). Fertilisers should not be considered harmless but weedkillers, wormkillers and fungicides can be decidedly dangerous and should only be opened for use *after* the instructions have been read. The instructions should then be observed faithfully.

Because of the risk of causing damage or of losing efficiency through inter-action, mixing of different chemical products, for example, wormkillers and fungicides, for ease of application is most unwise unless they are definitely known to be compatible. This is very rare.

The safest thing of all is to avoid having to use dangerous chemicals. Prevention is better than cure and sound maintenance can produce a good lawn which is virtually trouble free.

1

Some Basic Principles

Lawn turf; the soil below the turf; drainage.

1. Lawn turf

A lawn is a smooth area of ground covered with turf, generally beside a house. Turf may be defined as a ground cover of grasses and other plants growing so closely together and with vegetative parts, particularly the roots, so intermingled as to form a cohesive layer which resists tearing apart. A piece cut out of such a cover is referred to as a *turf* (plural *turfs* or *turves*). In a lawn turf non-grass plants are usually regarded as weeds.

There are many species of grass (150 to 160 are found in the British Isles) but not more than ten, characterised by their ability to withstand mowing, are likely to be found in a lawn. Even some of these are regarded as weed grasses. Some lawn grasses are able to spread by surface-creeping runners called stolons, and some have subsurface-creeping runners called rhizomes; some have neither and are sometimes referred to as bunch grasses (Fig. 1).

The grasses in a lawn reflect various things—the way the land was prepared, the kind of grasses planted, the kinds of grass indigenous to the district, the uses to which the lawn is put and, of course, its management, especially mowing. Grasses which might be used in lawn making are perennial ryegrass, timothy, smooth-stalked meadow-grass, rough-stalked meadow-grass and, of course, various kinds of fine fescues and fine bent-grasses.

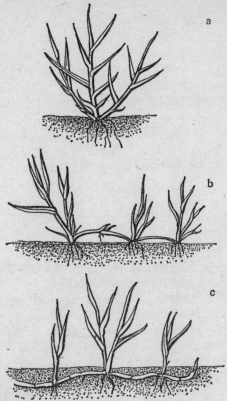

Figure 1   Different types of grass plant: (*a*) bunch type, (*b*) grass plant with stolon, (*c*) grass plant with rhizome.

Even these grasses vary in their ability to withstand regular mowing. Perennial ryegrass does not like mowing closer than 25 mm (1 in), timothy, smooth-stalked meadow-grass, rough-stalked meadow-grass and crested dogstail will tolerate 18 mm (¾ in) [possibly even 13 mm (½ in)] and only fine fescue and fine bent will survive the very close cutting [5 mm ($\frac{3}{16}$ in)] used on bowling greens and golf greens. For lawn purposes there seems little advantage in mowing down to the limits of what the sown grasses will stand so that even the finest and best maintained lawns should not be mown closer than 6 mm (¼ in) as measured by the setting of the mowing machine.

The kind of grass to plant on a new lawn depends in part on the kind of lawn that is wanted, but more on the skill and attention (work!) which can be put into the preparation and into regular maintenance afterwards. For a really fine lawn resembling a bowling green or putting green, only best-quality fine bents and fescues should be established on a very clean and well-prepared soil bed; for a medium lawn a proportion of smooth-stalked meadow-grass and/or timothy might be included with the fine fescues and bents, but only for drying lawns or paddocks getting little attention should perennial ryegrass be considered as well, even though it is such a useful grass on football fields.

Almost all lawns contain grasses which were not planted deliberately. These include some on the above list (which *could* have been planted if wanted) and others which are seldom used by choice. Yorkshire fog and creeping softgrass show up in patches of a different colour and texture which are difficult to eliminate. However, the most ubiquitous invader is *annual* meadow-grass which despite its name is seldom a true annual. There are very few areas of turf, no matter how high in quality, which do not contain a proportion of annual meadow-grass and since it will tolerate close cutting, much closely-mown turf on golf greens and bowling greens may have more annual meadow-grass than anything else. An important reason for the spread of annual meadow-grass is the fact that it can form viable seed under very close and very regular cutting, whilst even a lenient cutting regime inhibits seeding on the other grasses. Some of these may, however, spread by means of stolons or rhizomes.

A lawn commonly contains other plants, as well as grasses— the weeds. Any weeds found are, of course, those which will survive mowing. A weed may be defined as a plant growing in the wrong place and, whilst some people may like or at any rate tolerate plants such as daisies in their lawn, most people want an all-grass lawn, preferably free of weeds (including moss) and even of weed grasses.

At the surface of the lawn is the grass foliage and one tends to think of blades of grass growing vertically out of the soil like living brush bristles which need to be shorn off occasionally. This is too simple a picture. Between the leaf blades (not all of

which are vertical) and the soil is a zone of somewhat in-
definite thickness in which can be found recumbent leaves and
stems of the grasses plus stolons or rhizomes of some kinds of
grasses and even some root. Some of this material is very much
alive, some rather moribund and some dead. In general the
material is rather fibrous in nature and a moderate thickness
[say 6–13 mm (¼–½ in)] of fibrous material is desirable in that
it confers a wear-resisting soil cover and the resiliency which

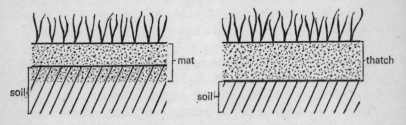

Figure 2   Cross-sections of turf showing mat and thatch.

makes the lawn feel like a thick carpet. An excessive thickness
of this fibre layer, for example, 50 mm (2 in) or more is referred
to as *mat* or *thatch*; it interferes with healthy grass growth and
may be a reflection of poor management. The terms mat and
thatch are sometimes used as if they were interchangeable but
they have, in fact, slightly different meanings. A layer of surface
fibre is thatch when it is mainly on the surface and not integrated with the soil and it is mat when it is partly or wholly
integrated with the topsoil. (See Fig. 2.)

Below the fibre is the soil with the main roots of all the plants
in the sward. The roots provide anchorage and are responsible
for the absorption of mineral nutrients and water. A good rooting system is very important for the production of a strong,
healthy turf which will tolerate regular defoliation and a good
deal of wear, and which will stand up to dry weather conditions
reasonably well. The soil should provide good conditions for
rooting and it has to be capable of yielding necessary supplies of
moisture and mineral nutrients, and also air since plants breathe
through the roots as well as through the foliage.

2. The soil below the turf

Many famous lawns are of great age and the householder who makes a lawn usually thinks of the construction as a 'once and for all' task. The soil below the turf is therefore a permanent feature—there are severe restrictions on what can be done to alter its physical nature or composition once the turf has been established. Important physical and chemical aspects of the soil are discussed below.

The physical nature of the soil

It is important to realise that the material in which the grass roots grow is not merely a solid mass. The soil consists of solid particles which may be mineral or organic in nature with pore space between them. The pore space, which may form about 50% of the total volume, is occupied by air and/or water. Also, the soil is the home of various forms of life including numerous micro-organisms (bacteria and fungi).

The mineral matter of the soil has been formed over the ages by the weathering of the rocks of the earth's surface. In it there are particles which vary in size from stones and gravel, through coarse and fine sand to silt and the very fine particles of clay. *Soil texture* reflects the proportions of the different sized particles and we can distinguish sandy soils, silty soils, clay soils, etc. In practice this is often done by rule of thumb but there are officially recognised laboratory procedures for accurate classification.

Soil organic matter arises mainly from dead vegetation and varies in nature from recognisable fragments of plant leaves, stems and roots through to dark coloured material known as humus which is commonly more or less fully integrated with the mineral part of the soil. The breakdown of plant remains into humus is brought about by various forms of life in the soil, ranging from earthworms to fungi and bacteria. Under turf, the soil commonly has a total of 5 to 10% organic matter by weight and this organic material plays an important part in producing the right physical and chemical conditions for satisfactory growth.

Most of the organic matter is found in the top layer of the soil—the topsoil. This varies in depth considerably but on the average it is about 150 mm (6 in) deep. The topsoil is comparatively rich in fertility and microbiological activity as well as organic matter, whereas the subsoil is much poorer in these things.

Under a lawn the soil usually has a very good crumb structure since grass roots represent one of the most efficient structure-forming mechanisms known. If the ultimate individual particles of a soil, the sand, silt and clay, were thoroughly mixed up as individual particles and compressed they would form a mass of solid material with no pore space for air and moisture (or grass roots!). Normally, however, these individual particles are grouped together in one way or another to form what is known as soil structure and a fertile soil, particularly one under grass, possesses what is known as a good crumb structure. The crumbs, which may be the size of lead shot or small peas, consist of aggregates of sand and silt loosely 'cemented' together by clay and/or humus. The existence of these irregularly-shaped crumbs results in spaces between them—pore space—being available for air and water. The soil crumbs are damaged by pressure or smearing (from feet or rollers) especially when in wet condition so that, on heavily-used winter pitches or much-rolled cricket tables for example, the structure may be completely destroyed and the pore space eliminated, with resulting ill effects on drainage, aeration, root formation and growth. Greenkeepers and groundsmen try to counter these ill effects by regular aeration but, since few lawns receive such severe treatment, comparable efforts from the lawn owner can be a complete waste of time.

The pore space in the soil should represent about 50% of the total volume and within the pore space good growth conditions are represented by about a 50:50 ratio of water to air. Grass roots need both water and air—excess of one means shortage of the other. Roots absorb water containing mineral nutrients in very dilute form during growth and the foliage transpires moisture in excess of requirements into the air. Grass roots also need air and, moreover, air in the soil is necessary for the correct functioning of soil micro-organisms.

Lawns can be established satisfactorily on most types of soil, the ideal probably being a sandy loam which drains freely and yet retains moisture to a reasonable extent so that the grass does not wilt every time it stops raining. In making new lawns it is worth making as much effort as possible to mix in ameliorants, or soil improvers, such as sand and organic matter to produce something like an ideal soil, bearing in mind that once the lawn is established the idea is never to see the soil again, let alone do anything with it! There is, in fact, little one can do to improve the physical composition of a bad soil below an existing lawn. Some of its adverse effects can be offset, for example, by aeration, but the most that can be done to change its composition is to try and work suitable material such as sand (for clay soils) or peat (for sandy soils) into holes made by a hollow-tine fork. (See p. 60.) On the other hand, by adopting a consistent policy of regular top dressing with compost material resembling a sandy loam, it is possible to build up over a period of many years a situation in which the lawn is growing in a layer of sandy loam overlying whatever existed originally.

Soil fertility
So far the soil has been discussed from the physical point of view which is so important. All too many people limit their interest in the soil to consideration of its chemical attributes and the relative value of different fertiliser treatments.

Soil fertility involves much more than merely having the right amount of mineral nutrients supplied by fertilisers. Aeration, moisture supplies, organic content and acidity are also involved. Moreover, of the many mineral nutrients required by grass for satisfactory growth, only three—nitrogen, phosphate and potash—commonly need supplementing. The special functions of 'the big three' are:

> *nitrogen:* promotes growth of leaf and stem and gives a good colour. It affects root growth since without sufficient top growth there is poor root growth, although too much nitrogen reduces rooting.
>
> *phosphate:* promotes root growth and tillering.
>
> *potash:* necessary to co-ordinate various growth processes and helps disease and drought resistance.

The big three are the main nutrients deliberately supplied in fertilisers although these may contain other useful elements also; the soil normally supplies sufficient of other necessary mineral requirements without special additions. Many soils indeed may contain quite large supplies of nitrogen, phosphate and potash, but in a form which is unavailable or very slowly available to the grass roots—hence the need for additional, more readily-available, supplies. One of the factors which affects the availability of mineral nutrients is the degree of soil acidity or alkalinity. Extremes of either of these opposites result in mineral nutrients being tied up in unavailable form, largely because of chemical reactions.

Soil acidity or alkalinity can be measured in a laboratory and the results are expressed in terms of a numerical expression —the pH. The pH scale may be used to describe the degree of acidity of solutions of any kind and ranges from 0 to 14 (extremely acid to extremely alkaline). Note that, although the expression *soil pH* is widely used, pH normally refers to solutions and not to solids. The usual range of pH for soils in the United Kingdom is about 4·0 (very acid) to 8·0 (very alkaline). For a good lawn a suitable pH would be between 5·5 and 6·0. If the soil becomes too acid (lime deficient) the turf becomes *unthrifty* (i.e. it does not thrive), susceptible to drought and, possibly, very spongy and even mossy. Over-acidity is corrected by sparing use of the right kind of lime. Carbonate of lime is the material to use and the correct amount depends on the degree of acidity and on the soil texture. A moderately acid soil may require only 70 g per m² (2 oz per sq yd) if it is sandy and perhaps 140 g per m² (4 oz per sq yd) if it is a clay, but expert advice is usually worth while. Where the soil is too alkaline coarse grasses, weeds, disease and earthworm activity may be encouraged. Correction of over-alkalinity is by no means straightforward. One has to rely on natural leaching out of the excess lime helped by the use of fertilisers which have a slightly acidifying effect, for example, sulphate of ammonia. It is, however, a common mistake to become too preoccupied with the pH aspect of maintaining a good lawn; very often the best pH is the one which already exists.

3. Drainage

There are two main aspects of drainage—getting the water through the soil and then getting it away. On all sports turf attention to both aspects is of the utmost importance although only the latter has received much attention until the last few

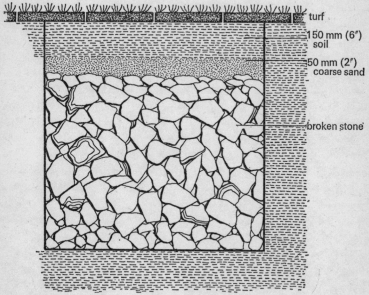

turf

150 mm (6″) soil

50 mm (2″) coarse sand

broken stone

Figure 3 Sump or soak-away for drainage.

years, i.e. most sports turf is provided with a pipe-drainage system. Experience indicates that most (though not all) lawns suffer remarkably little from drainage deficiencies caused by lack of drains.

Existing lawns

If an existing lawn is inclined to be wet the trouble may be mainly in the surface soil if this is of very heavy texture and/or is highly compacted. In such circumstances repeated aeration may bring about sufficient improvement.

Sometimes, however, it is essential to take steps to remove sub-surface water. On small lawns one or more soakaways or sumps positioned at the lowest part of the lawn may suffice. Such soakaways might be metre or yard cubes filled with stones, topped with gravel and/or coarse sand and finally covered with top soil and turf. (See Fig. 3.)

If this is not sufficient, one diagonal drain 600 mm (2 ft) deep can be placed right across the lawn, emptying into the soakaway

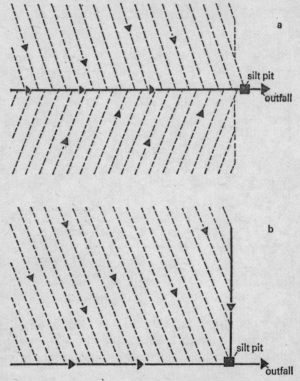

Figure 4 Typical drainage systems: (*a*) herringbone system, (*b*) grid system.

(or better still into a main drain if this is permissible). For very wet lawns and/or very large lawns a complete herringbone or grid system of drainage may be necessary on the lines illustrated. (See Fig. 4.)

If possible the main drain should be at a depth of 750 mm (2 ft 6 in) and the laterals at 600 mm (2 ft). Drains should be covered with gravel to within 200 mm (8 in) of the surface, followed by a 50 mm (2 in) thick 'blinding' of very coarse sand or fine gravel and then 150 mm (6 in) of topsoil and turf (Fig. 5). The subsoil should be taken away as it is excavated.

The actual drain-pipes may take the form of agricultural clay-ware pipes [75 mm (3 in) laterals, 100 mm (4 in) mains] or their modern plastic equivalents. Laterals should be joined to mains by means of purpose-made junction-pipes (Fig. 6).

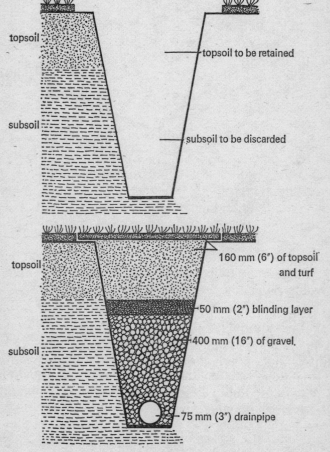

Figure 5 Section through lateral drain.

If, by good fortune, it is possible to connect to a public main drain it is wise, and often compulsory, to install a silt pit to collect mud from the water collected before it is discharged into the main drain (Fig. 7). Local authorities are often reluctant to accept drainage discharge into their drains and will usually make installation of a silt pit a condition of acceptance, if they accept at all.

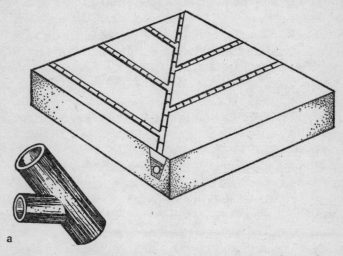

Figure 6 A herringbone drainage system with purpose-made junctions. (*a*) Clayware junction pipe.

Occasionally it may be necessary to install an interceptor or *catchwater* drain to trap water seeping in from adjacent land.

New lawns

When making a new lawn, thorough cultivation of both subsoil and topsoil plus physical improvement (e.g. by means of sand additions) of the topsoil are important to ensure free passage of excess moisture from the surface. If subsoil drainage by sumps or pipes is likely to be necessary then it is obviously prudent to install it during lawn construction.

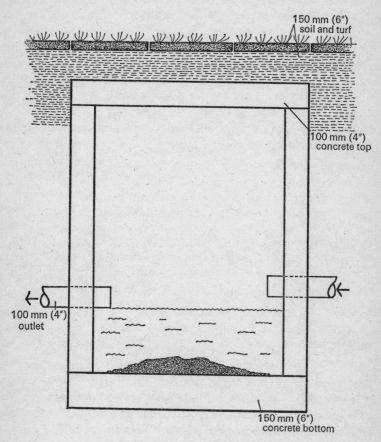

150 mm (6″) soil and turf

100 mm (4″) concrete top

100 mm (4″) outlet

150 mm (6″) concrete bottom

Figure 7 Section through a silt pit.

2

Making a New Lawn

Initial planning; constructional work; preparation of the soil; different methods of grassing down; early care of new turf areas; turf edging.

Essentially, making a new lawn simply involves planting grass on exposed soil but such a simple statement glosses over the many variations in site conditions and final requirements which actually occur. This chapter endeavours to help the keen lawn maker succeed in a variety of circumstances.

Initial planning

The procedure for making a new lawn depends on the nature of the site on which the lawn is to be made and on the kind of lawn it is intended to produce, taking into account how the lawn is to be used and looked after. A new lawn is sometimes made on an area which has been used as flower beds or vegetable garden and this situation creates few problems. It is possible, though extremely unlikely, that in moving into a newly-built house there is found to be a nice level piece of old pasture land with fine grasses which can be mown down to produce a really good lawn quickly and cheaply (quite a number of golf greens have, in fact, been made this way). If the pasture has coarse unacceptable grasses then a new start is indicated, the old turf being dug in or removed entirely according to circumstances.

Usually, however, the area for the garden and lawn around a newly-built house is in decidedly rough condition as a result of the builder's activities. Some builders are better than others in this respect but it is impossible for any of them to build a house without damaging the immediately surrounding area. They need to bring in and store materials; lorries and equipment have to cross the site, often when it is far too wet in horticultural terms. There is, therefore, a great deal of churning up which may mix up topsoil and subsoil (subsoil from the foundations may also be on the surface); there is usually a great deal of compaction of topsoil and subsoil and a variable amount of builder's rubbish. Sometimes the builder smooths out the site with all its 'warts' and covers it with topsoil which he has saved so that the garden area of the new house looks quite good but has, unfortunately, a lot of trouble covered up.

After examining the site and assessing its problems, thought should be given to, and decisions made on, the design of the garden as a whole, leading to decisions on the size, shape and contours of the lawn that is to be constructed. It is a mistake to try and produce a good lawn under the shade of large trees; even shrubs should be kept clear of the lawn as far as possible. It is therefore desirable to plan the design of the flower beds parallel with planning the lawn. Many people find a square or oblong lawn very attractive, especially since this is the most convenient shape to mow and it often fits the land available very well, but a lawn does not *have* to be square; some degree of irregularity in shape is often very attractive and allows variations in the width of surrounding flower beds. Even if a rectangular patch is decided upon, rounding the corners takes away the over-formal look and improves the general appearance.

There is no need to produce a perfectly horizontal area for the lawn. The lawn should be smooth but a sloping lawn will often be appropriate for a particular site and a slope helps drainage. A famous cricket ground has a slope of 1 in 40 which few seem to notice. There are pros and cons to having undulations in a lawn but, more particularly on large lawns, they are acceptable provided they are gentle and smooth enough to enable efficient mowing to be done. Water-collecting hollows should be avoided.

Flower beds within a lawn break up the grass area and make it look smaller. They also make mowing difficult and increase the amount of edging work necessary. Flower beds within the lawn area are probably more appropriate for very large lawns than they are for average domestic lawns. If lawns and flower beds are intermingled it is wise to avoid narrow strips of turf which attract all the wear and are difficult to mow except in one direction. Small areas protruding into flower beds can also be difficult to mow.

Many people regard lawns chiefly from the ornamental point of view but some want them dual purpose, for example, they want the back lawn to be used as a drying ground, and most parents put their children's welfare before the demands of a superior lawn. For first-quality lawns only fine grasses should be used but for dual-purpose lawns more robust grasses should be used as well. Preparation of the lawn is more or less the same for each type but clearly the standard needs to be higher if a first-class fine lawn is the aim.

Constructional work

The first step is to clear up after the builder and to take away all debris including tree stumps and roots and, if possible, any sub-soil which covers good topsoil, if there is any good topsoil left. If there isn't then it will be necessary to buy in topsoil, prefer-ably a sandy loam. If the builder has covered his rubbish and compacted earth with nice-looking topsoil it may be worth while taking it off again so as to put things right down below.

Grading the site to produce acceptable levels can be a major operation since only a very limited amount of level adjustment is permissible in the topsoil which must be left to an adequate thickness [say 150 mm (6 in)] and reasonably uniform to support a good lawn. Too much topsoil movement leaves some areas short of topsoil and some with an excess. Sometimes buying a load or two of matching topsoil to level up with is a worthwhile investment.

When the site needs a lot of level adjustment then the topsoil should be removed and level adjustments made in the subsoil.

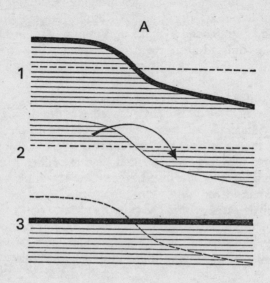

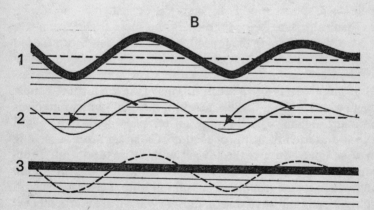

Figure 8 Grading by cut-and-fill. **(A)** and **(B)** show two different situations. In each case (1) represents the original situation, (2) levelling in subsoil after topsoil has been removed, (3) the final level after topsoil replacement.

This commonly involves a cut and fill procedure as illustrated (Fig. 8) but, again, on suitable sites bringing in suitable fill can save a lot of work. After grading the subsoil, all topsoil should be replaced and extra added to make up 150 mm (6 in) if there is a shortage. In confined areas requiring major grading it may be necessary to do the work in two halves so that topsoil can be placed on one half while the other is being graded.

The lawn need not be flat and often a fall of, say, 1 in 80 is beneficial in showing-off the lawn as well as in drainage. On sites with really steep slopes it may prove necessary to terrace the lawn area, that is to have the lawn at two levels with a gently-sloping bank between. Steep banks which are difficult to maintain should be avoided and in extreme cases a retaining wall may have to be considered.

If an existing tree within the proposed lawn area is to be retained (and this is *not* good for the lawn) then it is important for the tree that earth round the trunk should be retained at its original level by arranging a mound or large hollow as appropriate.

It is important to relieve compaction in the subsoil to as great a depth as possible and this may be done by digging or by mechanical means before returning the topsoil. Unfortunately the work of returning the topsoil, especially if done with the aid of mechanical equipment, can result in much compaction being restored and so further subsoil cultivation is commonly necessary. On relatively small areas, this may take the form of double digging (sometimes called mock trenching) which involves ordinary digging plus breaking up to spade depth the subsoil exposed as each trench is opened up. On larger areas subsoiling may be done through the topsoil with a tractor-operated subsoil cultivator. Even on fairly level sites with sufficient topsoil and where major grading in the subsoil is not necessary, subsoil cultivation is still advisable on most new lawn areas around new houses.

Topsoil and subsoil should be handled and moved only in reasonably dry conditions as otherwise the structure of the earth is damaged to the detriment of the lawn. This means, effectively, that the work should be done in the summer months.

As regards organising the new levels, most gardeners will be able to work things out sufficiently accurately for themselves —either by eye or by using strings, pegs, a straight-edge and a spirit-level—without too much elaboration. For some lawn sites the following procedure may be found suitable. A large flat-topped peg [say 50 mm (2 in) square] is driven into a convenient datum point with an exact measurement say 100 mm (4 in) left above the surface. Other pegs, which may be smaller [25 mm (1 in) square], are then driven in at measured distances [say 1·8 m (6 ft)] from the first peg and from each other to form a grid. These pegs are brought to true level with the aid of the straight-edge and spirit-level (or on really large sites with the aid of a Dumpy level or similar device). Where a horizontal lawn is required earth is adjusted so that it is to the same definite position at all pegs, but where a slope is wanted extra length as appropriate should be given to the pegs, for example, by placing blocks on the first pegs or substituting longer pegs, and the earth adjusted to a position relevant to the new pegs.

When subsoil and topsoil cultivation has been done adequately, few domestic lawns seem to show serious drainage faults, but where necessary a simple drainage system can be installed on the lines mentioned in Chapter 1. The best time to put in pipe drains is usually after topsoiling and subsoil cultivation.

If the work described above is completed in early summer a short period of fallowing is possible before sowing or turfing at the end of the summer. If the work uses the whole of the summer then the earth can usefully be left in the dug state over the winter to allow for settlement and for the topsoil to benefit from frost.

Preparation of the soil

When the whole depth of the topsoil has been dug over or mechanically cultivated, the next step is to break down the clods. This is usually most conveniently done by trampling with the feet followed by repeated cultivating with a hand or machine cultivator. A roller may be used to break dry clods but it can be very hard work manoeuvring it! It is important to ensure that no large unbroken lumps are left in the topsoil because they may lead to settlement later and this means, of course, an uneven lawn. During these initial preparations of the soil it is often advisable to work in materials to improve its physical composition. Thus on a really sandy soil it is worth while to improve its moisture and plant food-holding capacity by thoroughly mixing in granulated peat or other suitable organic material at a rate of at least 3·5 kg per m² (7 lb per sq yd). If the soil is on the heavy side generous applications of suitable sand should be well worked in. It is now recognised that the much-quoted term 'sharp river-washed sand' can be very misleading and cause the use of sand which is not really very suitable because it is too coarse. A good sand is a medium sand with particles which are predominantly of one size in the range 0·5–0·2 mm and a sand such as this might be found among sands conforming to zone 3 or zone 4 of British Standard 882 for fine aggregates. However, in making a new lawn, within reason the quantity of sand is probably more important than its quality in terms of particle size. The sand should preferably be lime-free since even a small percentage of lime in material applied at heavy rates can have such a marked effect on the quality of the lawn. Depending on the precise texture of the soil generous applications may mean as much as can be afforded, 120 kg per m² (2 cwt per sq yd), or even more, may be desirable but smaller amounts are worth while if not mixed in too deeply. If a rotavator is used for mixing sand with heavy soil there is liable to be a compacted layer resistant to water penetration at the depth to which the machine works and it is advisable to loosen this with a fork or with other cultivating equipment without turning over the soil.

No matter which method of grass establishment is used, the soil bed must be brought to a firm, fine tilth—always working in near-dry conditions. The surface should be well raked with an ordinary garden rake, and stones and other debris collected. Some firming-up can be achieved by rolling but this is liable to leave air pockets which lead to uneven settlement later. The best procedure is to progress slowly over the site in *very* short steps with all the weight on the heels so that soft spots are firmly filled (Fig. 9). After this, rake over and repeat both the treading and raking, taking off any stones which appear. At the end of the process the earth should be so firm that heeling causes no more than very shallow depressions but the soil should not be so compacted that water will never soak through it. The surface should, of course, comply with the final levels intended, should

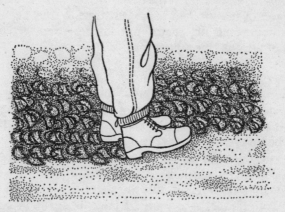

Figure 9   Heeling to achieve satisfactory firming of the soil bed.

be perfectly smooth and should be clear of stones with any measurement of 13 mm (½ in) or more. In the final smoothing out, a lute such as the proprietary Trulute can help considerably and the same tool can be used later for working in bulky top dressings. During all the lawn cultivations, special attention should be given to ensuring good and free-draining soil conditions on areas which are liable to receive particularly heavy wear (such as any relatively narrow spaces between flower beds) so as to help these areas to stand up to their punishment.

The soil usually contains seeds and viable portions of weeds and weed grasses which will mar the new lawn unless they are eliminated. It is possible to ensure a clean soil bed for the lawn by chemical sterilisation but this is not really practicable for amateurs. The best procedure is to have a period of fallowing, preferably most of the summer. This means cultivating out the weed plants at regular intervals as they show themselves. An alternative to killing the weeds by cultivation is to spray them with a non-persistent chemical preparation such as one based on a mixture of paraquat and diquat. Remember that this preparation is extremely toxic and supplies should be kept in their original containers and locked-up well away from children. The operation of fallowing can, to some extent, overlap the final soil preparation work described.

The end of the summer is the best time to start off the grass, typically the end of August for sowing grass seed and the month of October for laying turf.

Different methods of grassing down

Turf can be initiated by planting stolons of creeping grasses but this procedure is seldom adopted in the United Kingdom where commercial supplies are difficult to obtain.

Lawns are usually made either by laying turf or by sowing grass seed.

The main advantages of turf are that one can see in advance the kind of turf that is to form the lawn (it should be bought on the basis of samples), a good green lawn is produced very quickly and weeds are less likely to pose problems. Moreover, it can be laid in late autumn when it is too late to sow grass seeds. Unfortunately supplies of good turf, whether from old pastures or specially grown, are difficult to come by and much of the material available to householders may not be worth laying, despite its high cost. There is a British Standard Specification for turf for general landscaping but the standard is more appropriate for road verges than for good lawns! Sea-marsh turf, which is still popular for bowling greens, usually proves very disappointing when used for making lawns since it commonly deteriorates in a year or two, the original fine grasses being superseded by unwanted invaders and weeds. When examining samples of turf points to note are the soil it is growing in (it is unwise to surface the lawn with clay), the fineness of the grasses, the absence of weeds and the amount of fibrous material in the base (too much means built-in problems and poor rooting, too little may mean that the turf breaks up with handling so that there is much wastage). The chosen turf should be supplied to a uniform thickness of, say, 37 mm (1½ in).

For those who want really good turf quickly there is now a seedling 'turf' available in patented form. Such turf is produced in a short growing period of six to twelve weeks (if necessary from a purchaser's selected seeds mixture) in one of two ways. The seedling turf which came on to the market first is grown on a polyurethane foam laid over a watery sludge of various suitable materials which are left behind when the turf is sold. The second type is grown on a thin layer of special soily rooting medium overlying an impenetrable base (originally polythene but now sometimes very heavily rolled earth). Material supplied from either process is very light and easy to handle, being only about 13 mm (½ in) thick, and it can be laid by rolling it out like a carpet if necessary. The turf is held together by the foam layer and/or the densely intermingled roots. It may also be reinforced with plastic mesh. In price seedling turf is about the same as good, normal turf.

Laying turf to a satisfactory standard requires the exercise of a good deal of skill and care and is somewhat laborious, so that even if good turf is available many people prefer to sow grass seed and this is, of course, much cheaper. A higher standard of soil bed preparation is, however, necessary when grass seed is to be sown, particularly as regards eliminating weeds. Laying turf can cover up a multitude of sins and if the children and pets cannot be kept off the new lawn then it is almost essential; they won't hurt newly-laid turf very much but they are liable to churn up a beautifully prepared sown area before it has established sufficiently to withstand this kind of wear. The chief drawback to turfing remains the difficulty of obtaining good turf at a price that is acceptable.

Choosing a seeds mixture can provide problems particularly as there are so many apparently conflicting advertising claims. Usually seed is bought as a proprietary mixture with an attractive name and reliance is placed on the reputation of the firm concerned. This is all right within limits but many firms sell several different lawn seeds mixtures at different prices and the buyer has to decide which he wants. It is important to buy a mixture of the right type for the purpose intended. Three main types may be distinguished :

TYPE 1 :   High quality mixtures for first-class fine turf.
TYPE 2 :   General purpose lawn seed mixtures without perennial ryegrass.
TYPE 3 :   General purpose lawn seed mixtures which contain perennial ryegrass.

For all three types there are very good new varieties (*cultivars*) of the species contained and varieties which are not as good. The good varieties of each species cost more than the poorer varieties so that, having decided upon type, it should be worth while to buy the most expensive mixture within that type. There is, however, no such thing as the perfect seeds mixture.

Few people are qualified in, or concerned with, making up their own seeds mixtures but there is no great problem if sufficient basic information is available.

Type 1 mixtures vary comparatively little from the well-known mixture of :

> 70 or 80% Chewings fescue
> 30 or 20% browntop bent

With this mixture a sowing rate of 35 g per m² (1 oz per sq yd) is recommended.

Type 2 mixtures vary more in their composition but a useful formula is :

> 30% Chewings fescue
> 25% creeping red fescue
> 10% browntop bent
> 35% smooth-stalked meadow-grass

A suitable seed rate for this type of mixture is 25 g per m² (¾ oz per sq yd).

Type 3 mixtures vary a great deal in their composition, especially the low-priced ones. A good one can be made up from:

    20% Chewings fescue
    20% creeping red fescue
    10% browntop bent
    20% smooth-stalked meadow-grass
    30% perennial ryegrass

A seed rate of 17 g per m² (½ oz per sq yd) is probably sufficient with this type of mixture.

Other grasses which might be included to the extent of 10–20% in Type 2 and Type 3 mixtures include timothy, rough-stalked meadow-grass and crested dogstail. Some seed merchants supply special mixtures for shady situations. These usually contain wood meadow-grass which, in the wild, tolerates shade quite well but does not often persist in a regularly-mown lawn. If a lawn is required in a shaded situation the best advice seems to be to sow the same mixture as would otherwise be used and mow it much less short than on an open site.

Type 1 mixtures as described above may be used for fine lawns mown down to 5 mm ($\frac{3}{16}$ in) if necessary but are better at 6–13 mm (¼–½ in). Type 2 mixtures are suitable for play lawns or drying lawns and for mowing down to 13–19 mm (½–¾ in), while Type 3 mixtures for mowing at 19–25 mm (¾–1 in) or more may be considered suitable for utility lawns which receive much hard use (or abuse).

Whatever mixture is decided upon it is worth while to obtain the best available cultivars of the various species.

Planting stolons

The most common grasses to be established by this method in those parts of the world with a temperate climate are creeping bent (*Agrostis stolonifera*) and, in sub-tropical areas, Bermuda grass (*Cynodon dactylon*). There are various ways of planting stolons but the most common way is probably to chop the stolons into 50 or 75 mm (2 or 3 in) lengths, scatter these thinly on the fully-prepared soil bed, cover lightly with topsoil or compost and then roll them down.

If no soil space larger than about 25 mm (1 in) square is left and the surface is kept moist, new shoots and roots soon develop and the formation of a lawn all of the same grass is well on its way. Frequent top dressing is advisable and mowing should commence when the grass gets long enough. Hand weeding may be necessary until a good surface cover is obtained.

Turfing the lawn

If (and only if) the soil is too acid or lime deficient, as shown by soil tests, an appropriate amount of ground limestone, say 140 g per m² (4 oz per sq yd) should be deeply raked into the soil at any convenient time during the later stages of preparation. Fertiliser treatment may also be guided by soil tests but, unless the soil is known to be rich after growing vegetables, a suitable pre-turfing fertiliser will usually be necessary. This may be a proprietary product or, alternatively, a home-produced mixture as follows could be used :

	per 100 m²	or	*per 100 sq yd*
fine hoof and horn meal	3·0 kg		6 lb
fine bone meal	3·0 kg		6 lb
powdered superphosphate	3·0 kg		6 lb
sulphate of potash	1·5 kg		3 lb

The fertiliser should be spread as uniformly as possible and well raked in.

Although turf can be laid at almost any time of the year provided that it can be watered in dry weather until well rooted, autumn is undoubtedly the best time. The soil should, however, be reasonably dry when turfing takes place to facilitate good workmanship without soil damage.

The chosen turf should be delivered in suitably-mown condition and, for making a good job, the best size of turf is 300 mm (1 ft) square. Some people, however, prefer larger pieces, e.g. 450 mm × 300 mm (1½ ft × 1 ft) or 900 mm × 300 mm (3 ft × 1 ft). The turf should be uniform in thickness of the depth arranged which might be 38 mm (1½ in) or 32 mm (1¼ in). If turf of uneven thickness is accepted it is most desirable to even it out by *boxing*, i.e. by laying the turf, grass-side down and roots upward, in a shallow box or tray of the appropriate depth and shaving the turf down to the depth of the box by means of a stout knife drawn across the top edge of the box (Fig. 10).

Turf should be laid as soon as possible after delivery, especially if it has to be stacked, since it may deteriorate within a few days. If turfing is delayed then it is wise to take down the stacks, lay the turf out flat (preferably in a shady position) and keep it moist by watering as necessary.

It is usually a good idea to start turfing by laying at least one turf width completely round the borders of the lawn. The work should then be continued by working from one side in such a way that no disturbance of the prepared soil is involved, that is the new turf is laid from planks placed on already laid turf (Fig.

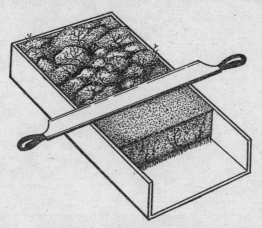

Figure 10 Boxing turf to even thickness.

11). Turf supplies should also be barrowed to the point of laying on planks suitably organised over laid turf. The actual laying may be done with a garden fork but there is much to be said for laying by hand from the kneeling position. Individual turves should be laid in the same kind of pattern as bricks in a wall and they should be pushed tightly together as they are laid. At the end of each row there is likely to be a space requiring only a short length of turf. It is unwise to put a small piece at the edge; instead, the last complete turf should be put up to the edge and the space behind it filled in with a piece of turf cut to size (Fig. 12). Beating down (as often seen on road verge work) is *not* recommended and any unevenness should be rectified in the earth below by addition or subtraction as appropriate.

When turf laying has been completed the lawn area should be lightly rolled [e.g. with a garden roller not over 250 kg (5 cwt) in weight] and then top dressed with sandy compost material as described in the section on top dressing. The top dressing should

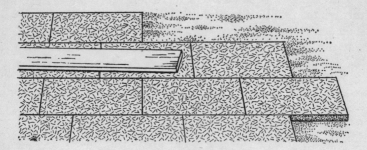

Figure 11   How to lay turf.

be applied as evenly as possible (possibly with a shovel) at a rate of 1·5 to 2·5 kg per m² (3–5 lb per sq yd) and then well worked into the surface by drag mat, drag brush or lute so that it smooths out the surface and gets worked into the crevices between turves. Top dressing may need to be repeated at least once after a few months.

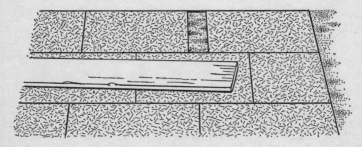

Figure 12   Procedure at the end of a row of turf.

If the new seedling turf is used instead of traditional turf it is very important to observe suppliers' instructions very carefully. Because of its lightness larger pieces of this kind of turf can be handled conveniently but remember that the larger the pieces, the more difficult it is to ensure accurate laying to levels. Two particularly important points to watch with this kind of material are, firstly, that it should not be laid too late in the autumn because it is too delicate to withstand severe weather before it has rooted down and, secondly, that it should not be laid at times of the year when dry weather is likely unless regular and frequent watering can be really relied upon.

Mowing of turfed areas should commence at only moderate severity as soon as there is sufficient growth to justify the operation. The height of cut can then be gradually lowered until the appropriate cutting height is reached.

Sowing grass seeds
As when turfing, if the soil is too acid it should be limed appropriately. Again, if the land is known to be rich no fertiliser is likely to be needed but on new sites a proprietary pre-seeding fertiliser, possibly a relatively cheap granular preparation, may be used. The enthusiast can save a little money at the expense of some effort by making up a good mixture from straight fertilisers on the following lines:

	per 100 m²	or	*per 100 sq yd*
sulphate of ammonia	1·5 kg		3 lb
fine hoof and horn meal	1·5 kg		3 lb
dried blood	1·5 kg		3 lb
powdered superphosphate	3·0 kg		6 lb
fine bone meal	3·0 kg		6 lb
sulphate of potash	1·5 kg		3 lb

The well-mixed material should be spread immediately after mixing and distributed as evenly as possible before being carefully and thoroughly raked in. There are advantages in allowing a week or so to pass before sowing the grass seed but in practice little detriment may be expected if, for convenience while the weather is right and the land in good condition, sowing follows straight on.

When seed sowing is carried out the land should be in raked condition and quite dry near the surface but, preferably, slightly moist below. Although seed distributors can be bought or hired, hand distribution is usually better and more convenient. The sowing should be done on a still day and even distribution is helped by dividing the seed into two equal proportions and sowing in transverse directions, for example, one half in a north–south direction and the other half in an east–west direction. On fairly large areas it is worth while dividing up the area into measured sections of, say, 20 m² or 20 sq yd, weighing out the seed for each section into two lots and then sowing each section separately in two directions. The enthusiast may even divide the area into metre or yard squares either by making a complete network with string or by stringing out at metre or yard intervals and then measuring out successive metres or yards with a measuring stick. The seed for each square can be conveniently collected in a small container which holds the right weight. It is quite a good idea to sow seed a short distance beyond the intended boundary of the lawn to ensure, after trimming in due course, a fully-grassed edge, and it is prudent to reserve a little seed for over-sowing any thin or bare patches which may later appear in the body of the lawn. If a machine is used for sowing, dividing the seed into two halves is still worth while. (See also the section on spreading fertilisers.)

The seed should be carefully raked in. It should not be buried too deeply lest it lacks sufficient strength to reach the surface and so rots away. On the other hand, the seed does need a light cover; seed left right on the surface might shrivel up in dry conditions just after germination. Rolling as the final operation is seldom an advantage.

Particularly in urban areas birds can cause serious problems in the first two weeks or so. Grass seed can be purchased ready treated with bird repellent but this, though useful, does not provide the complete answer since much of the damage caused by birds is due to them scratching and dust-bathing rather than eating seed, while the seed rates used allow a little for the birds! Probably the most effective deterrent is a temporary grid of black cotton stretched tightly over the lawn and supported about 75 mm (3 in) from the ground by short sticks.

From time to time over a period of some forty years or more, different firms have marketed pre-sown sheets or rolls of 'carpet' of paper or some other suitable material. Such products do not seem to confer any great benefits and they seem to have been very little used. Using them usually involves preparing the soil bed in the ordinary way, laying out the pre-sown material and pinning it down before lightly covering with topsoil or compost.

The grass should appear in about two weeks after ordinary sowing if the weather is favourable. Watering the seed bed is not recommended as it is better to rely on nature to start the grass off, but once it has germinated careful, gentle watering is advisable if the weather is then dry.

When the grass is sufficiently high [50 mm (2 in) for the fine mixtures, 75 mm (3 in) for coarse mixtures] any worm casts should be swept off and visible stones removed. The area should then be lightly rolled to firm up the soil around the grass roots so that the young plants are not disturbed by mowing, to encourage tillering and to push any remaining small stones into the surface so that they do not get into the mower. When the grass has retained the vertical (i.e. when it stands up again after being somewhat flattened by the roller) it should receive its first cut. Use a very sharp mower with the blades set high so as to remove no more than a third of the grass. At this stage conventional side-wheel mowers and rotary mowers are very useful in that they do not have the front roller to press the soft grass down before the cutter reaches it. Over a period of several weeks, according to progress, the mower blades should be gradually lowered until the cutting height required is reached.

Early care of new turf areas

It is extremely important to ensure first-class attention for the new lawn in the first year of its existence or what may be called the development year.

Turfed lawns

If the work of establishment was efficiently done at the right time and good turf used there should be few problems. Lawns which have been turfed often need a spring fertiliser after autumn/winter turfing and, to ensure a smooth surface, two or three top dressings applied at suitable intervals are beneficial. Regular mowing is essential and a close watch should be kept for disease. When turf is laid out of season, i.e. spring or summer, regular watering is necessary in dry weather. If weeds have been imported with the turf and selective weedkilling becomes necessary this should not be carried out until the turf is really well established, well rooted and growing strongly, though odd weeds can of course be removed by hand at any time.

Lawns sown with grass seed

For new lawns established from seed the first year is particularly critical. The aim should be to give maximum encouragement to the sown grasses so that they will become dense and keep out invaders. The sooner there is a good, well-established cover of grass, the sooner the lawn can be used, but even with the best of management it should not be walked upon very much for about a year. During this period it is beneficial to encourage growth by periodic dressings of fertiliser (mainly nitrogenous) in the right weather conditions and according to season. It is wise not to take the grass on fine lawns down to the final height of cut until surface smoothness has been ensured by top dressing at intervals with compost. A close watch for disease attack should be kept up right from the beginning. In the first few weeks damping-off disease may attack the seedlings but usually only when they are growing too close together or when the soil is cold and wet. There are both pre-emergence and post-emergence diseases. Attacks by pre-emergence diseases become evident only when the grass fails to appear. A possible precaution against them is to use seed which has been treated with appropriate fungicide but, in fact, this is not often done. There are appropriate fungicides for treating post-emergence damping-off, but the best approach to all possible damping-off problems is to use the right seed rate on a well-prepared seed bed in good conditions at the right time of the year.

Any selective weedkilling which proves necessary should be delayed as long as possible until the new turf is really well established. Normal selective weedkillers should certainly not be used before the lawn is three months old and preferably quite a lot later. In the early stages it is usually well-worth-while hand weeding the occasional perennial weed or coarse grass plant, but annual weeds need not cause too much worry since they die out under the influence of mowing. If perennial weeds become a problem in the early stages because of inadequate preparation, then a special lawn weedkiller based only on the chemical ioxynil may be used carefully according to maker's instructions.

Turf edging

If metal-strip edging is used it is probably most convenient to install this after the new lawn is well established and the edges trimmed to their final position. Wood edging could also be installed at this time or before establishment, but concrete edging with concrete haunching support is best put in before soil-bed preparation is completed.

So that the turf can be mown right to its edge, the permanent edging should be a little lower than the surface and so should any surrounding footpaths if possible. For the same reason the turf should be kept at least a short distance from walls or other raised obstructions (including footpaths).

3

Routine Maintenance of Established Lawns

Mowing; lawn edge trimming; top dressing; fertiliser and lime treatment; mechanical operations; watering.

Owning a lawn should give great pleasure. The aim of this section of the book is to help in understanding the lawn's needs and thus to minimise the amount of work necessary to maintain the lawn to the standard wanted.

Maintenance requirements are rather demanding but at the same time fairly simple. They are demanding in that *regular* attention is necessary; in particular mowing *must* be carried out as frequently as there is growth to justify it. On the other hand, in general a lawn owner does not need the vast technical knowledge which some seem to consider necessary, nor is there any need for the *regular* expenditure of effort and money on all kinds of treatments which might only prove necessary in some special cases.

Indeed, there are probably almost as many good lawns spoiled by their owners trying too hard as there are lawns spoiled by neglect. *Once a lawn has been established to an acceptable standard it is often possible to maintain it so almost indefinitely by very little attention other than regular mowing!*

A good lawn is characterised by uniformity in all respects. It should be uniform in colour, texture and surface smoothness, and free from blemishes in the form of weeds, disease and worm casts. It needs to be sufficiently durable to withstand whatever degree of wear is required of it and it should have a good colour throughout the year. Clearly these matters have to be interpreted in terms of personal aspirations and requirements which may vary considerably—from a lawn like a bowling green to the small paddock or orchard where tidiness with minimum effort is the aim.

Mowing

Whatever the standard aimed at, regular mowing is essential to give anything like a reasonable lawn. Therefore a good lawn mower in good condition is very important.

Mowing equipment

For very small patches of lawn in front of small terrace houses some people make do with garden shears. These perform most satisfactorily if they are cared for properly and kept sharp. At the other end of the scale, small paddocks which need only to be kept reasonably tidy (even if grazed) may be mown conveniently with a machine with a cutter bar (like an agricultural mower), with a flail-type cutter or with a large rotary mower; a large motor mower of the conventional cylinder type might be appropriate if a slightly higher standard was required for the paddock. For the unenergetic, aged or infirm there are ride-on mowers of various types which are suitable for large paddock work.

The choice of mower for the average lawn owner is remarkably wide and even confusing. Moreover, buying mowers has much in common with buying motor cars—personal choice comes into the matter as well as performance and price. When buying a mower it is wise to bear in mind not only the quality of mowing required but also the size of the lawn and the presence or absence of banks in it, storage facilities available and the convenience of getting the mower from its home to the lawn and back—lifting a heavy mower up steps or over flower beds can be very difficult.

For small lawns a hand mower of the conventional kind is probably most appropriate. Such mowers may be of the side wheel or of the roller type, the latter being preferred so as to avoid scoring the turf and to facilitate mowing of the lawn edges. Unfortunately, hand mowers capable of giving a bowling green finish are difficult to come by but there are models suitable for both the medium- and the low-standard lawn.

Powered mowers are popular because they reduce the effort required to mow the grass.

Rotary mowers, which have fan-like blades rapidly revolving on a vertical shaft driven by a petrol or electric engine, are remarkably widely used despite the slight bruising effect they have on the tips of the blades of the grass. They do not have a bottom blade but can be adjusted for height of cut. There are various sizes and types available, including one that behaves rather like a hovercraft in that it is air-borne in use. Rotary mowers are remarkably versatile and can be used for almost any type of lawn but, to date, there is no rotary machine which will produce a really fine finish.

Conventional mowers may be powered by petrol motors or by electric (mains or battery) motors (Fig. 13). The motor may drive the cutting cylinder only or may provide locomotion as well. The range of types, quality and price is considerable; there is a machine to suit most pockets but obviously the better machines which give a good finish and are very reliable cost more than inferior machines. For a bowling-green-type finish the chosen machine should have ten or twelve blades and give 155 cuts per metre run (140 per yard). The height of cut range might be 3–19 mm ($\frac{1}{8}$–$\frac{3}{4}$ in). For lawns where such a high standard is not the aim then mowers giving rather fewer cuts per unit of length are satisfactory. Some conventional mowers can be fitted with brushes or combs to assist in reducing the amount of procumbent growth.

The best mowers, whether conventional or rotary, have a container for collecting grass cuttings. The container should be light but sufficiently large for convenience and sufficiently strong to have a long, useful life. It should be easily removed from, or replaced on, the machine. The arrangements for delivering cuttings into the container should be satisfactory.

Whatever kind of mower is used, it will perform better if

it is properly cared for. After use the machine should be thoroughly cleaned and checked before being put away. Grass cuttings should be brushed off and all grass removed from the grass-box. It is wise not to use the mower in wet conditions, but, if it is so used, hosing down may be the most efficient way of cleaning it. Any plant stems which have become wound round

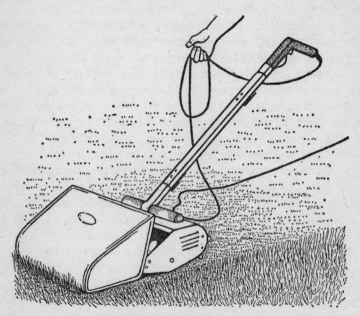

Figure 13   An electric mower.

the axle should be got out by the most convenient tool (e.g. a screwdriver), and the machine should be inspected for loose nuts and bolts and for wear and tear which needs action. Lubrication of all appropriate points following the manufacturer's instructions may be performed before use or after use—or both! This simple job merits far more attention than it usually gets, since lubrication is vital to ease of operation, the life of the machine and efficiency. With powered mowers the motor must also be maintained, and lubrication as appropriate is also important here. In the case of petrol engines the air cleaner needs regular checking for cleanliness, the sparking plugs should be kept clean and correctly adjusted and the correct oil level must be maintained. Where there is a chain drive this should be checked regularly to ensure the correct tension.

With mains electricity powered mowers, the safety aspects should not be forgotten; cable handling arrangements during mowing need to be carefully systematised and the cable should be examined carefully at regular intervals to see that the insulation is intact. If a mower is battery powered then clearly the battery merits and needs regular attention, especially maintaining acid levels and charging as required.

Although grass should be mown at any time of the year when there is sufficient grass to mow, in practice there is usually in effect a 'close' season in the winter months when the mower is put in store. Before putting it away it is wise to try and ensure that it comes out in good working order the following spring. For all mowers this means a good clean-up and thorough lubrication. With due care for the fingers, cutting blades should receive a coating of oil from an oily rag, a paint brush or one of the new oil sprays which are very convenient to use. Grass-boxes and thrower plates should be painted after cleaning down with a wire brush or other suitable equipment as necessary.

Motors also require attention. With petrol motors, important points are to drain the fuel tank, to take out the sparking plugs for cleaning before replacing, to close the throttle lever thus relieving the load on cables and to leave the engine on the compression stroke. To achieve the latter, the starting rope should be gently pulled until maximum resistance is felt, this indicating that the piston is at or near the top of its travel. Batteries of petrol motor mowers and batteries of battery/electric mowers should normally be removed and stored fully charged in warm surroundings. All mowers should, if at all possible, be stored in a really dry place, preferably on a wooden floor or wooden staging. Fertilisers and other chemicals, which might also be in storage, should be kept well clear of the mower since they are likely to start corrosion.

Finally, if the mower needs repairing or sharpening this work should be organised in good time at the end of the growing season so that the machine will be ready for action in the spring.

A conventional-type mower which is sharp and well set will cut a piece of paper cleanly. Delay in getting the machine attended to may mean that the machine is not available in good order when it is needed most. It is a great pleasure when at the first spring cut the mower performs straightaway as if it had been in regular use.

Effects of mowing
The quality of a lawn is conditioned mainly by the type of mowing coupled with its frequency and regularity. Mowing affects the growth habits of the grasses, their root and shoot development and the botanical composition of the sward. Within limits mowing encourages tillering and thus a dense sward, but for each of the common lawn species there is a height of cut below which they survive with difficulty, if at all (see Turf).

The weed population is also affected in amount and type by mowing. If a lawn is cut too keenly for the grasses contained in it then weeds can invade the weakened turf. The types of weed in the lawn are those which can survive under the cutting conditions prevailing. Only low-growing weeds withstand regular cutting and these include rosette types (like daisy and plantain), types with surface runners (such as the clovers), types with underground runners (such as yarrow), the mat-forming types (such as pearlwort and chickweed) and, of course, the mosses. Note that a mowing machine is non-selective in the sense that it cuts all vegetation down to the height chosen whereas grazing animals are usually selective in their defoliation.

Height of cut
Since the height of mown grass is very difficult to measure, the cutting height is usually described in terms of the bench setting of the mower. When a conventional mower of the roller type is used the *height of cut* is the distance between a straight-edge placed so as to pass from front to back roller and the cutting edge of the bottom blade (Fig. 14). With side-wheel mowers and ordinary rotary mowers the straight-edge is laid from roller to side wheel. A useful device for measuring height of cut can be made from a wooden straight-edge into which is screwed to the required amount a screw with a flat underside. The distance be-

tween screw and wood measures the height of cut (Fig. 15). A metal bar with a threaded bolt and winged lock-nut is even better. The bolt is adjusted to give the required cutting height between the bolt head and the bar and then locked in position. When using these devices the screw head or bolt head can be 'hooked' on the bottom blade and the mower adjusted to bring the straight-edge to touch the front and back rollers.

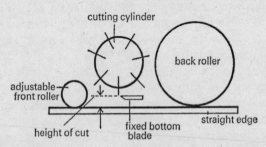

Figure 14   Height of cut as measured on the mower

Since uniformity is such an important requirement for any lawn, careful setting of the mower is required to ensure that the desired height of cut is achieved for the whole of the cutting width.

Different heights of cut favour different grass species in the sward. Very low heights [below 5 mm ($\frac{3}{16}$ in)] weaken all grasses and encourage some types of close-growing weeds like pearlwort and especially moss. Cutting too high encourages the coarse grasses which tend to smother the fine grasses and produce a thin open turf in which upright weeds such as dandelions may become established.

The best height at which to cut an existing lawn depends very much on the grasses present. Even the best-quality lawns consisting entirely of fine grasses need to be cut no lower than 6–13 mm ($\frac{1}{4}$–$\frac{1}{2}$ in). The average lawn might reasonably be cut at, say, 13 mm ($\frac{1}{2}$ in) or so but for ryegrass-dominant swards used as drying areas 25 mm (1 in) might sometimes be appropriate. Longer cuts, such as 50 mm (2 in), are unusual for

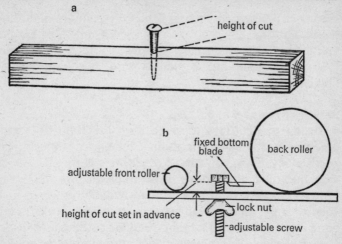

Figure 15 Setting height of cut (a) a simple mower gauge and (b) using a special mower gauge.

lawns but might be considered appropriate for the turf in the orchard or paddock.

The heights of cut referred to above refer to the main mowing season. It is usual, more particularly on closely-mown turf, to allow the grass to be a little longer from autumn (as growth falls off) to spring (as growth gains momentum). Thus very fine turf mown normally at 5 mm ($\frac{3}{16}$ in) is, during this period, kept at about 8 mm ($\frac{5}{16}$ in).

When adjusting the mower to leave the grass a little longer, allowance should also be made (if necessary) for the softer surface conditions which often result from increased moisture at this time of the year. Softer conditions allow the rollers or wheels of the mower to sink into the surface sufficiently to make an appreciable difference to the actual height at which the grass is cut.

Frequency of cut

Regular cutting is most important but the frequency required depends on the kind of turf. Fine turf needs cutting as often as two or three times a week (or even more) during the height of the growing season, but once a week or three times a fortnight often proves sufficient for a less fine lawn. Less frequent mowing is needed at times when there is little growth but even during the winter cutting should not be neglected if mild weather causes unusual but appreciable growth. Only by regular and sufficiently frequent mowing can a good lawn of adequate density be obtained and maintained.

Return or removal of cuttings

Allowing the cuttings to remain on the lawn as a regular practice has some advantages and some disadvantages. An important advantage to many lawn owners is that it does away with the chore of disposing of boxes of cuttings which can be rather laborious, even though these will rot down to make a good organic compost for general use in the garden. Perhaps more important is the fact that when the cuttings are allowed to stay on the lawn lesser quantities of nutrients are removed from the site. Moreover, the drought resistance of the turf is increased. There are, however, definite disadvantages. The cuttings may contain seeds of ordinary weeds or weed grasses and usually, allowing the cuttings to fly, results in an increase in these undesirables (in the flower beds as well as the lawn!) and also leads to a softer turf which is less durable and more prone to disease. The mineral plant foods contained in the cuttings are released to the soil only when the clippings rot down. Decaying organic matter is a first-class food for earthworms and so allowing cuttings to fly encourages earthworm activity. Earthworms perform some useful functions but earthworm casts spoil the appearance of a lawn, create muddy surface conditions in wet weather and favour weeds. The casts (which may contain weed seed from below the surface) smother or weaken small areas of grass and provide good seed beds for any weed seeds they contain or which are blown or carried in (on shoes or mower) from elsewhere.

For most lawns the balance of the pros and cons is such that, as the regular procedure, boxing off the cuttings is advantageous. In prolonged drought conditions, however, if water is not available then allowing what meagre amount of cuttings there are to fall on the lawn forms something of a protective mulch which may be worth while.

Practical tips on good mowing practice

It is preferable to mow often but not too closely rather than to cut very closely at intervals of two or three weeks as this weakens the turf. A good clean cut is obtained more easily and with less expenditure of energy and time if the surface is dry when mown. Moreover, grass cuttings which are short and dry fly into the grass-box more easily than do long, wet cuttings and it is worth a little effort to try and achieve a dry mow.

The weather can't be controlled but one can vary the time or day of mowing. If the lawn is wet from rain or dew, switching

Figure 16 The attractive striped effect produced by a good conventional mower.

or brushing to disperse the droplets on the foliage will help considerably especially if it can be done an hour or two before mowing on a drying day. In any case, any earthworm casts should be dispersed before cutting the grass.

Mowing should be done in a smooth up and down manner over the length or width of the lawn leaving attractive stripes (Fig. 16); it should not be done in a series of short, sharp, backward and forward bursts which are bad for machine and for lawn. Turning at the end of each run should be done most carefully, possibly off the lawn altogether where practicable, so as to reduce wear. Despite practical difficulties which may arise on small-sized or peculiarly-shaped lawns, changing the direction of mowing frequently is a good plan. If the grass is always mown in the same direction there is a tendency for some types of turf to form a pile or nap, i.e. for the grass all to lay in one direction. Indeed on most lawns there is a tendency for some of the grass to become laid (although not necessarily in one direction) and occasional brushing or light raking followed by mowing helps the retention of the smart appearance which results from dense vertical growth. If the mower is suitable it may be worth while having a purpose-made brush or wire rake fixed to it so that at every mowing the procumbent growth is brought up to the mower.

Particularly on larger lawns always mowing in the same up and down direction may lead to 'washboarding', i.e. the formation of irregular waves on the surface, made up of lines of slightly high and slightly low parts as on an old-fashioned washboard. Changing the direction of mowing minimises the risks of incurring this problem.

If a conventional mower is not correctly set for clean cutting then the grass blades may be chewed rather than cut. This may prove detrimental to the health of the turf as well as its appearance. When the mower is set too low, having regard to the smoothness and regularity of the surface, then high spots may be mown so closely as to be scalped, i.e. the turf is skinned off to reveal the earth below. If the grass is too long for the machine setting then a cylinder mower may cause a ribbing effect. This effect is produced by close lines of longer and shorter grass with an appearance reminiscent of the ribbing in some types of knitted garment.

Uneven cutting may also be caused by uneven setting of the mower with one end cutting shorter than the other, or by damage which has been incurred by the cutting cylinder or bottom blade. Mowing across the slope of a lawn with a marked fall also causes uneven cutting since the weight of the mower pushes the lower end of the cutter closer to the ground than the higher end. Mowing up and down the slope is probably the only answer to this problem. Using rotary mowers eliminates some of the above problems, but the quality of finish that a good cylinder mower confers may also be lost.

A possible alternative to mowing
Scientists have for many years turned their attention to finding chemicals to stunt grass growth and so minimise mowing. There are now some commercial products available for use as sprays to check grass growth but there are limitations to the usefulness of such materials and to date they do not seem to have earned a place in ordinary lawn management.

Lawn edge trimming

When a lawn has been mown its appearance is greatly improved if the grass growing over the edges is trimmed. A pair of garden shears may be satisfactory for the very small lawn but for the larger lawn something less back-breaking is well worth while. Long-handled shears are very convenient, not too expensive and have a very long working life (Fig. 17). Purpose-made edge trimmers are even easier and more convenient to use.

When a lawn edge tends to wander a little and extend into adjacent areas it may be trimmed with a straight spade or with a half moon (Fig. 18). The necessity for this operation can be avoided by the installation of fixed edging of timber, concrete or aluminium strip. With a fixed edge regular trimming consists merely of cutting the straggly growth which stretches beyond the edge, with the advantage of a firm line to follow.

Top dressing

In lawn management top dressing means the application of bulky material like sandy compost, spread as evenly as possible at 1·5–3·0 kg per m² (3–6 lb per sq yd) by hand or with a shovel and then worked into the sole of the turf by suitable equipment such as a drag brush, drag mat, lute or even simply the back of a wooden rake (Fig. 19).

Purpose of top dressing

A smooth surface with uniform growth is an important characteristic of a good lawn. A smooth surface looks good and it permits the grass to be mown at a uniform height, i.e. without longer grass in the hollows and shorter grass on the bumps. This is particularly important on fine lawns but even lawns which

Figure 17   Edge-trimming with long-handled shears.

are of medium or low quality look better when they have a smooth surface.

Initial preparation of a new lawn to produce a smooth, firm soil bed for the seed or turf planted, has a considerable bearing on the smoothness of the finished product, but there is always room for improvement when the lawn has become established, especially in the first two or three years. Rolling will achieve some smoothing out of an uneven surface but in doing this it also causes compaction which is detrimental to root growth and drainage. Professional groundsmen and greenkeepers produce surface smoothness by top dressing and the amateur is well advised to adopt a similar approach.

The primary purpose of top dressing is to smooth out the surface, but a good top dressing material has value also in providing

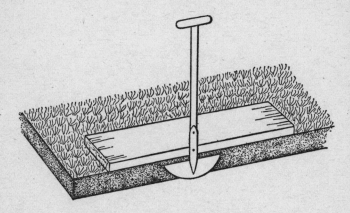

Figure 18   Trimming lawn edge with half-moon edging iron and wooden straight-edge.

some plant nutrients (applying it in September/October helps winter colour), improving surface resiliency and improving the nature of the immediate surface soil. Top dressing in dry weather provides a mulch which minimises moisture loss through evaporation.

Top dressing material

The ideal material for top dressing is a special form of sandy compost produced by making a compost heap with alternating layers of sandy soil and rotted farmyard manure and allowing it to stand for a year or so before breaking down and mixing with suitable sand to produce material with the right sandy texture. Obviously this procedure is not very practicable for the lawn owner who, like many professionals, needs to make up an acceptable substitute. This might well take the form of a mixture of:

> 6 parts suitable sand
> 3 parts sandy loam soil
> I part granulated peat

The sand for this mixture should be a lime-free medium sand preferably with particles in the size range 0·5–0·2 mm and

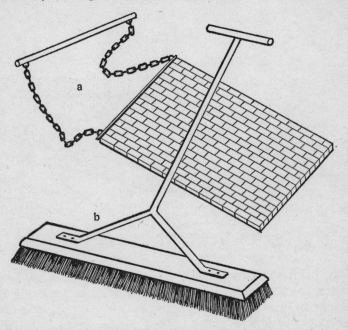

Figure 19 Tools used for working in top dressing: (*a*) drag mat, (*b*) drag brush.

coarse sand should be avoided (compare sand used for soil improvement when making new lawns).

Good, clean (weed-free) sandy loam should be obtained for the mixture if possible but other types of soil can be used with suitable adjustment of the proportion of sand added, i.e. less sand for a sandy soil, more sand for a heavy soil. Really heavy or clay soil should be avoided since it is almost impossible to produce a good uniform friable mix from them.

Organic matter for the mix is conveniently provided by crumbly granulated sphagnum or sedge peat, but other organic materials such as leaf mould may also be used, again possibly with an adjustment of the proportions shown; for example, the leaf mould may be of a decidedly soily nature so that the proportion of sand may need increasing.

Thorough mixing of the ingredients in near-dry condition is important to ensure uniformly friable material which should be passed through a fine screen [5 mm or 6 mm ($\frac{3}{16}$ or ¼ in)] before use. The soil may contain seeds of weed grasses or other weeds and even the sand and peat may not be entirely weed-free, so that buying sterilised materials, especially sandy soil, is well worth while. Few lawn owners have the enthusiasm or the space even for substitute compost making and it is likely to prove most convenient to use commercially produced and sterilised top dressing if it can be obtained without too much trouble or cost.

Top dressing with sand alone or peat alone is not recommended since it can result ultimately in the formation of layers as in a sandwich cake and this layering is detrimental to root development, to drainage and to drought resistance. By regular use of the right kind of top dressing mixture it is possible over a period of time to reach a position where, whatever the original nature of the soil, the turf is being grown in what should be near-perfect topsoil!

Applying top dressing

The most convenient time to apply top dressing is early autumn while some growth persists. Top dressing may, however, be carried out at any convenient time in the growing season when the grass will push its way through and anchor down the compost. It is unwise to top dress in the winter months when there is little or no growth.

The top dressing material should be in near-dry condition when put on and should be spread on a dry surface during weather likely to remain dry for sufficient time for the top-dressing operation to be completed by thoroughly working the compost into the surface. The amount of top dressing material to use depends on individual circumstances, especially on the relative smoothness or otherwise of the existing surface, the vigour of the turf and the height to which it is mown (it usually pays to mow immediately before top dressing). An average dressing might be 2·0 kg per m² (4 lb per sq yd) and it should be well worked into the surface by whatever method is most convenient, the idea being to smooth out the surface by depositing less material on the high spots and more in the hollows but avoiding excess which might lead to smothering or encourage disease. On small lawns top dressing may be smoothed out and worked well into the turf by means of the back of a straight wooden rake or by means of a home-made lute consisting of a piece of board fixed at a suitable angle to a long handle. It is, of course, possible to buy purpose-made lutes and, at least on large lawns, drag mats or drag brushes (not ordinary brooms) are very useful. A 2–4 m (6–12 ft) straight-edge of wood or metal is a further help in guiding towards a first-class surface—indeed it can in some circumstances itself be used to smooth out the top dressing. Clearly one top dressing cannot be expected to produce a perfectly smooth surface on an area which is markedly uneven, but repeating the operation once or twice a year for several years can confer amazing benefits. Once a lawn has been smoothed out it may not need regular top dressing unless wear interferes with surface smoothness.

Fertiliser treatment

The need for fertiliser
The fertiliser requirements of existing lawns are markedly variable. Some lawns established on fairly rich soil may grow very satisfactorily for many years with scarcely any fertiliser treatment at all and the occasional dressing of complete fertiliser (say once every five or ten years) may be all that is necessary. Other lawns, especially closely cut very fine lawns from which cuttings are removed or lawns which receive heavy wear, may need at least one suitable feed each year, particularly on hungry soil. Because of the wide variation in requirements, the pressures of commercial promotion and the often conflicting

advice of the countless 'experts' which exist in the press and in the neighbourhood, it is in this aspect of lawn maintenance that lawn owners often make mistakes. There seem to be two main classes of lawn owner : those who over-feed considerably (possibly with the wrong type of fertiliser) and those who never feed at all. Of these the latter often have the better lawns !

Keeping up a reasonable level of mineral nutrients in the soil by means of fertiliser treatment does help to keep the turf dense and of good colour so that it is attractive in appearance and it is unfortunate that extra growth usually means more mowing. This should automatically guide the lawn owner in the right direction, i.e. to avoid over-feeding and give as little as is consistent with producing sufficient growth. It should also be remembered that those who do not box off their cuttings have less need to feed than those who do, although the latter are likely to have the better lawns. Conversely those who want a lawn like a bowling green and therefore mow frequently (and very closely) and box off cuttings may find the turf unthrifty and of poor colour unless they give it as much feed as a bowling green gets.

The kind of fertiliser to use

Few lawns need more than one dressing a year and this may conveniently take the form of a balanced complete fertiliser (i.e. one containing the three main mineral nutrients, nitrogen, phosphate and potash, in suitable proportions) in spring. For those few who wish to make up their own mixture the following formula will suit average conditions :

	per 100 m²	or	per 100 sq yd
sulphate of ammonia	1·5 kg		3 lb
fine hoof and horn meal	0·5 kg		1 lb
dried blood	0·5 kg		1 lb
powdered superphosphate	2·0 kg		4 lb
fine bone meal	0·5 kg		1 lb
sulphate of potash	0·5 kg		1 lb

Thorough mixing is required immediately before use and in addition it is recommended that the whole of the fertiliser be bulked up (diluted) with near-dry sandy compost or similar material to facilitate spreading and minimise scorch risk. The

amount of sandy compost to use is about 14 kg per 100 m²
(28 lb per 100 sq yd) and once again thorough mixing is needed.
In some circumstances adding calcined sulphate of iron at 0·5 kg
per 100 m² (1 lb per 100 sq yd) to the above mixture is beneficial
in improving grass colour and checking weeds and disease.

If growth falls off during the summer then it can be stimulated by applying a simple nitrogenous fertiliser treatment as a
tonic, e.g. sulphate of ammonia [8–17 g per m² (¼–½ oz per sq
yd)] mixed with sandy soil [140 g per m² (4 oz per sq yd)] once or
twice during the growing season, but preferably no such tonic
should be given after the end of August.

Nitrogen is the most important mineral nutrient in the maintenance of a lawn and, indeed, where supplies of available
phosphate and potash in the soil are reasonably satisfactory any
feeding the lawn is given may take the form of nitrogenous
fertiliser alone, either as sulphate of ammonia only or as sulphate of ammonia plus dried blood and/or fine hoof and horn
meal, bulked with compost of course, e.g. 8 g sulphate of ammonia, 8 g dried blood and 8 g fine hoof and horn meal mixed
with 140 g compost per m² (¼ oz sulphate of ammonia plus
¼ oz dried blood plus ¼ oz fine hoof and horn meal plus 4 oz
compost per sq yd). In this mixture the sulphate of ammonia is
quick acting, the dried blood almost as quick but longer lasting
and the hoof and horn meal is slow acting and long lasting. It is
usually unwise to apply fertilisers rich in nitrogen after the end
of August because of the risk of encouraging disease.

It is as important to use the right kinds of individual fertilisers
as it is to use any fertiliser at all and the materials mentioned
above are all satisfactory. To avoid weed, worm and disease
trouble it is wise not to use fertilisers which leave an alkaline
residue such as nitrate of soda or nitro-chalk (except in excep-
tional circumstances) and to avoid excessive use of organic
fertilisers. A good fertiliser should have a blend of inorganic
and organic constituents, the latter being of particular value in
spreading out the growth response over a longer period than
would be obtained when quick-acting inorganics are used alone.
New synthetic products designed to supersede organics and
provide a steady growth response over several weeks or months

have been marketed in recent years but the perfect material has not yet been produced. Some of the new products are, however, blended in to various proprietary lawn fertilisers.

Because of the apparent complexity of lawn feeding coupled with the difficulty and trouble in mixing and handling fertilisers to the formulae mentioned above most lawn owners choose the easy and convenient way out—they buy ready-mixed fertilisers

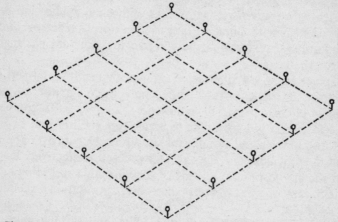

Figure 20 Preliminary division of the lawn for hand distribution of fertiliser.

as proprietary products. When this is done it is important to buy reputable brands of lawn fertiliser and to use them exactly as recommended by the maker, for example at the recommended rate in the right season.

Spreading fertiliser

Whatever kind of fertiliser is used, spreading should be done most carefully to obtain even distribution. Uneven application results in uneven appearance and growth and may even produce severe scorch on patches which receive excess fertiliser. Such patches may, indeed, be killed off entirely or they may die later as a result of disease attack on the damaged but over-fed turf. An intelligent handyman can ensure even distribution of fertiliser by hand distribution, having first divided the mixture into at least two equal portions (by weight) to be spread in two transverse directions (e.g. north–south followed by east–west). For large lawns further subdivision is advised so that there are two equal portions for every 50 m² or 50 sq yd. Subdividing into even smaller patches has advantages for some. Nowadays many people buy or hire small distributors but over-confidence in these can be misplaced. They need to be used with the utmost care if they are to make a reasonable job. It is necessary to go up and down the lawn in regular fashion and give great attention to matching up successive widths. As with hand application it is a good plan with standard (linear) types of spreader to divide the fertiliser into two and apply in two directions at right angles (Fig. 21).

Spinner-type distributors often pose difficulties in getting uniform distribution since they apply more fertiliser in the middle of their spread than they do at the edges. To compensate for this it is a good plan to divide the fertiliser into two as before and to spread at half rate but with each pass overlapping half the previous pass (Fig. 22). This procedure effectively levels out the application. With this type of machine spreading half-rate in each of two transverse directions can result in a chequer-board effect.

With any fertiliser distributor, filling and turning must be carried out with the greatest possible care and, indeed, when important areas are being treated it is often better to go off the area concerned or to have a large sheet on which to turn. Some kind of marking-out arrangement is desirable whatever procedure is used for fertiliser application and possibly stringing out is the best—that is, dividing the lawn into equal parts with string.

Fertiliser is best spread in a dry period during showery weather. The surface should be dry and the soil moist when the treatment is applied—spreading in rain or when the lawn is wet can be a messy and unsatisfactory operation. On the other hand, if the fertiliser stays on the surface too long it may cause scorch even though it has been spread efficiently. If no rain falls within one or two days of the application careful, gentle but ample watering-in is advisable to avoid damage to the grass. It is unwise to apply fertiliser during drought conditions. If for special reasons (such as ensuring a smart appearance for a particular

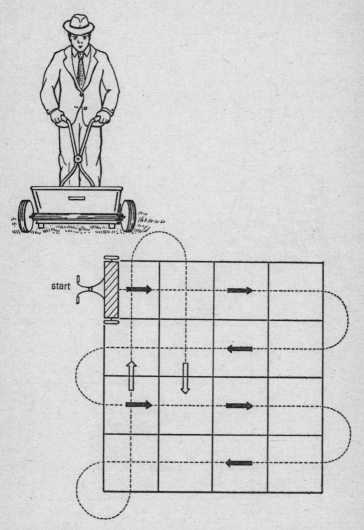

start

Figure 21   How to use a linear-type fertiliser distributor.

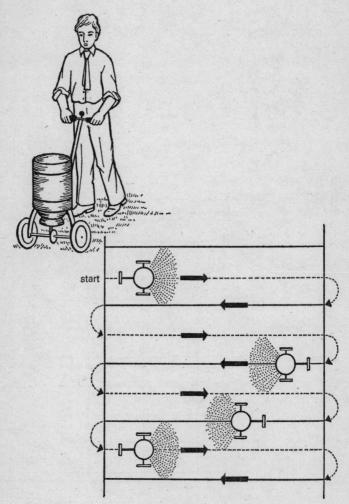

start

Figure 22 How to use a spinner-type fertiliser distributor.

occasion) this has to be done then the soil should be thoroughly moistened a short interval before the application, leaving time for the surface to dry, and watering-in should be undertaken immediately afterwards.

If distributors are to give good service they need very careful looking after. They should be thoroughly cleaned and lubricated after use. Before use, it is wise to check that they are working properly and to calibrate them by making test runs with the fertiliser on a smooth surface, perhaps over pieces of paper of unit size, since fertilisers vary considerably in density and in freedom of flow; even the same fertiliser might run through differently on different occasions according to its 'condition' on the day.

Liquid fertilisers

In recent years there has been some interest in the use of fertilisers designed to be applied in solution but it would seem that these have limited value in lawn maintenance, partly because the need for solubility and compatibility restricts the

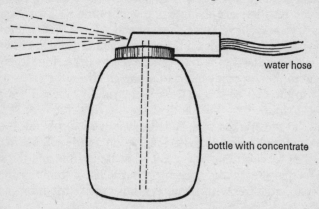

Figure 23 An appliance for liquid fertiliser.

kind of fertiliser which can be used and partly because of the difficulty of ensuring that every bit of turf gets the same amount. Uniform application of solutions by sprinkler or watering can is very difficult. Spraying on relatively concentrated solutions can cause damage by scorch and within the lawn there will be some unevenness in the rate at which sprinkled water infiltrates various areas because of compaction or an uneven surface. Quite useful results can be obtained however with the equipment shown in Fig. 23. The stream of water in the hose-pipe draws up concentrated solution from a vessel and dilutes it considerably so that it can be applied through a fine rose as a shower over the area of the lawn which, immediately afterwards, can be watered with the same equipment after the fertiliser solution has been used up.

There are, however, still solubility and compatibility restrictions on the types of fertiliser which can be used to make up suitable fertiliser solutions, even the proprietary ones, and visible effects from liquid fertiliser are usually short lived.

Liming and the lawn

Lawns very rarely need lime. Lime is needed to correct excessive soil acidity when this occurs but excess of lime encourages weeds, earthworm activity and fungal dieases. Even when the soil gets too acid so that the vigour of the grass and its reaction to added fertiliser are reduced the application of lime, though necessary, may have some detrimental effects. When lime is applied to a lawn it falls on the surface and thus makes the surface alkaline. It takes a long time, even years, before leaching of lime to the lower layers or to drainage brings the surface pH down to the desired levels. Only if the results of a soil test and the behaviour of the turf both show the need for lime should liming be undertaken and, indeed, it is wise to obtain expert advice before liming. (See also the section on the soil below the turf.) The form of lime to use is carbonate of lime and the best time to apply it where necessary is in the late autumn or in the winter months. As with fertilisers, uniform distribution is important.

Mechanical operations

Much mechanical treatment is involved in efficient maintenance of the turf on golf greens, bowling greens and cricket tables but such treatment may be of very little importance for the average domestic lawn. Indeed any benefit conferred may not be worth the time and effort put into the work which may even have harmful results.

Scarification

For intensively maintained and used sports turf, particularly fine turf, regular surface scarification with spring-tined wire rakes (Fig. 24) or, more commonly these days, with mechanical scarifying equipment, is necessary to groom the turf and produce good playing surfaces which permit and encourage skilful play. Few lawns need the same amount of intensive treatment. Occasional brushing with a drag brush or stiff broom or light raking, by bringing up horizontal growth, helps to keep a lawn looking trim and to prevent the formation of an excessive layer of fibrous material at the surface. In addition to bringing up to the mower recumbent grass leaves, stems and surface runners, scarification brings up runners of weeds like clover to be mown off and therefore restricts the spread of such weeds. With some mowers light scarification can be achieved by fitting a purpose-made wire rake to the mower on a more or less permanent basis.

A very old lawn (usually of fine grasses) which has developed a mat or thatch of fibrous material may need more severe treatment involving vigorous use of a wire rake or, for ease and effectiveness, the prudent use of a mechanical scarifier in which rotating knives or rotating wire rakes are power-driven. Such severe treatment should be carried out when good growth conditions are assured so that growth will restore the surface. Usually late summer or *early* autumn prove the most appropriate times to do this kind of work. Lawn owners who have a severe problem with excess fibre will probably try and borrow or hire a mechanical scarifier and it is wise to make arrangements in advance since the machine may be booked up when it is wanted in September.

Aeration

Most sports turf needs some form of aeration frequently. This is partly to offset the compaction caused by play, rolling and so on, and partly to encourage rooting which on bowling greens, for example, is restricted by the very close mowing imposed.

Few lawns are subjected to the same stresses. It follows that much of the effort put into spiking and forking is wasted and indeed, may be harmful since every hole made in the turf makes it so much easier for weed grasses and weeds to become established.

However, if there is soil compaction, poor surface drainage or a shortage of root then aeration of some kind to a sufficient

Figure 24   Spring-tine wire rake.

depth may well be advantageous. Much good work can be done with an ordinary garden fork, particularly on small, wet patches (Fig. 25). It is better to use the fork reversed, so that it faces in the opposite direction to that of normal use. After forcing it in with the foot it should be given a gentle forward and backward leverage to expand the holes just a fraction without disturbing the turf surface.

Special turf aerating equipment does the work rather more satisfactorily. For the small- or medium-sized lawn so-called hand forks (Fig. 26) are best but aeration machines may need to be used on larger lawns. Aerators may have solid tines which are round or flat in shape, or hollow tines which remove cores of soil. When cores are taken out the holes attract new roots and also allow the surrounding soil to expand which, of course, relieves the compaction. Good root development is, of course, necessary to sustain a good healthy turf and increase its resistance to drought and to wear and tear. Attempts to brush sand into the holes so as to confer some permanent improvement in

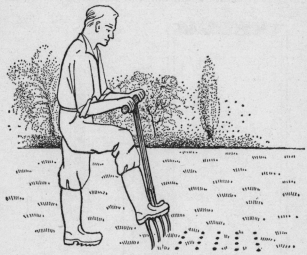

Figure 25   Aeration with a reversed garden fork.

water penetration may be worth while on heavily compacted or clay soils.

Hollow tining has obvious advantages where it is needed but it also has disadvantages. Over-use may result in a soft, weedy turf and even on bowling greens and golf greens it is usually done only once every three years or so. (It is seldom or never done on cricket tables.) Solid tines do not relieve compaction in the same way as hollow tines do but they certainly facilitate the passage of air and moisture into the soil and give some assistance to rooting while, at the same time, they do not have such a marked effect on invasion by weed grasses and weeds. Moreover, solid tines can be used very frequently (e.g. once a month, although once a year is probably ample on most lawns) without producing an unwanted softness in the surface.

When aerating the soil it is important to do this to sufficient depth—say 100–150 mm (4–6 in). For this reason some of the equipment bought by householders is of very little value for aeration, although it may be useful in the summer to prick the surface so as to assist penetration of rainfall or applied water.

The time to carry out normal aeration work is usually the autumn when ground conditions are sufficiently moist and soft

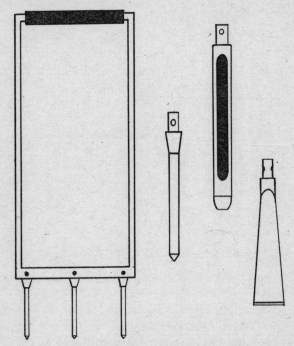

Figure 26   A lawn aerating fork with interchangeable tines.

to enable the work to be done effectively without too much effort. If it is done before growth ceases it can be followed up with top dressing which will to some extent be pushed into the holes as the material is worked into the surface of the turf.

Rolling

If a lawn needs rolling it is usually difficult to borrow a roller because, fortunately, so many people have now realised that a roller is *not* an essential piece of equipment for lawn care and there are few rollers about! Rolling causes soil compaction resulting in impeded air and water penetration and in restricted root growth. This harms the lawn and makes extra work necessary. Rolling does help to smooth out the surface but at the cost of increased compaction, and generally little or no rolling is required on lawns. Possibly a light rolling may be advantageous in the spring to firm up any upheaval caused by severe winter weather but usually a conventional roller-type lawn mower operated with the cutter held up will do all that is required.

Watering

The drought resistance of a lawn depends on the grasses contained, on the extent of root development and on the physical and chemical attributes of the soil.

The need for water

Grasses vary somewhat in their tolerance of water shortage. At one end of the scale fine fescues are considered quite drought resistant while at the other end annual meadow-grass is decidedly susceptible. A well-developed rooting system enables grass plants to explore a greater volume of soil to obtain moisture and thus resist the dry weather for a longer period. As regards the soil itself, very sandy soils which are low in organic matter soon dry out while soils with a high humus and/or clay content have a much greater capacity for moisture retention (although not all of this is available to plant roots). Where the soil has available nutrients in reasonable (but not excessive) supply, turf will stand up to dry conditions quite well. On the other hand, when the soil is too acid the turf is particularly susceptible to drought.

Most lawns will survive without watering even in very dry summers and, indeed, withholding water in dry weather may sometimes have long-term advantages in weakening the less desirable grasses such as annual meadow-grass. In the short term, however, weakening of any grass in the lawn causes discoloration and disfigurement so that if a green, pleasant appearance is to be maintained, then watering may be called for.

If watering is to be undertaken at all, it is advisable to start watering before the soil dries out to the extent that the turf starts showing ill effects, and to water adequately. This means giving sufficient water at each watering to moisten the soil thoroughly to full root depth and not merely moistening the surface. It is wise to do this at intervals of a few days so that the surface can dry out in between. Keeping the surface permanently wet promotes shallow rooting and encourages disease attack. As a rough guide to the amount of water to give, it can be assumed that the *maximum* requirement in severe drought is 25 mm (1 in) of water (25 litre per m² or almost 5 gal per sq yd) every ten days. Excessive watering can lower the quality of a lawn and encourage invasion by disease and moss.

The best kind of water to give is pure rainwater which is at air temperature, but since the main requirement of water is that it should be wet most people use mains water for their lawn, regardless of any drawbacks it may possess. However, hard water (i.e. water containing lime) should be avoided if practicable since quite a lot of lime can reach the lawn in the water during a season's watering and this encourages weeds, worms and disease.

Application of water

Applying water by means of a watering can is a laborious chore even on a very small lawn, although it does avoid the charge imposed on hose-pipes by some water authorities. Watering of small lawns and grassy banks may be conveniently undertaken by means of a hose-pipe fitted with a fine rose but, for any reasonably sized lawn, some kind of sprinkler arrangement (Fig. 27) is advantageous in ensuring gentle and fairly even application. There are various types of sprinkling equipment and it is important to ensure that hose connections and so on match. Other important points to consider when buying equipment are:

(*i*) It should be easy to carry from store to lawn.
(*ii*) It should be simple to set up, to adjust and to operate.
(*iii*) It should enable the whole area to be watered as evenly as possible.

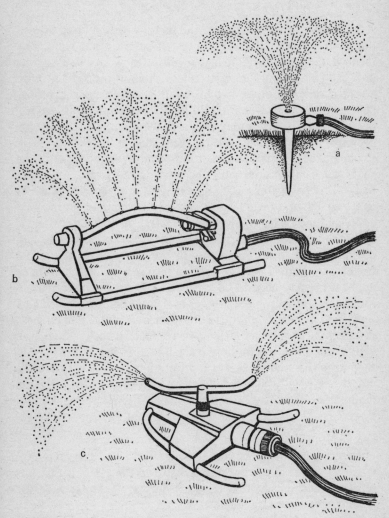

Figure 27 Three types of lawn sprinkler: (*a*) simple static, (*b*) oscillating, (*c*) rotary.

(iv) It should produce droplets simulating moderate rainfall.

(v) It should not leak and so cause ponding.

Sometimes, especially when the turf is rather matted and/or the lawn has been allowed to dry out before watering is commenced, there can be difficulty in getting the water to penetrate into the soil. In such circumstances shallow pricking as with a spiked roller or other suitable equipment can be of considerable assistance. If water will still not penetrate and the soil below stays dust-dry it may be worth while using a fairly easily available biodegradable wetting agent such as Synperonic NDB. (Biodegradable materials are decomposed by bacteria, etc., and so do not persist in the soil.) The procedure is to apply 0·5 litre in 100 litres of water per 25 m² or 1 pint in 25 gallons of water to 25 sq yd of affected area. The solution should go in quite easily and should be followed immediately by generous watering with the sprinkler. Alternatively a proprietary soil penetrant could be used in accordance with the directions given. Some washing-up liquids may be pressed into service but the rate of application may need to be increased a little. However, within limits the strength is not critical and *providing the washing-up liquids do not contain any additives such as bleaches which are detrimental to the turf* all will be well. Nevertheless, it is prudent to try them out on only a small area in the first place and then keep this under observation for a few days to see that it is not detrimentally affected before proceeding to treat the remainder of the lawn. Once the lawn is well wetted further trouble is unlikely if regular watering is kept up as necessary.

Fertiliser need after watering

There are many who consider it necessary to give *extra* fertiliser when a great deal of watering is done, on the grounds that lots of plant food will have been washed away. There seems little justification for extra fertiliser on an ordinary lawn in these circumstances unless vast excesses of water have been given or, of course, if the turf has become weak because it has been receiving insufficient water!

An alternative to watering

If it is not possible to water during dry weather the turf may be assisted by conserving existing moisture through mulching. Allowing the cuttings to fly gives some mulching effect though during dry weather there aren't many cuttings. Light top dressing with sandy compost is, however, of great benefit in these circumstances.

4

Lawn Troubles

Fungal diseases; pests; weeds; miscellaneous problems.

From time to time the lawn owner has problems with the lawn, and the nature of these and how to deal with them is described in the following pages. As I said earlier, these have much in common with a home-doctor book: the long list of possible ailments is rather frightening but, fortunately, as with the home-doctor book, the patient is not, nor likely to be, cursed with them all.

Fungal diseases

There are several fungal diseases which attack intensively-maintained turf. They include fusarium patch disease, corticium (or red thread) disease, typhula blight, dollar spot disease, melting out disease and ophiobolus disease. Sensibly managed domestic lawns seem to be little troubled by these diseases but, of those listed, the first two, fusarium and corticium, are the most frequently encountered and will be discussed here. Disfigurement or damage from fungi known as basidiomycetes may also occur. Fuller information on all these diseases is to be found in *Fungal Diseases of Turf Grasses* by N. Jackson and J. Drew Smith published by the Sports Turf Research Institute.

Fusarium patch disease
Fusarium patch disease is caused by the fungus *Fusarium nivale*. It occurs most frequently during mild, moist weather at almost

any time of the year but especially in the spring and autumn, particularly the latter. The first signs are usually small irregularly-shaped yellow patches (often overlooked) which in the 'right' conditions grow larger and darken in colour through reddish or bright brown (when the disease is at its most active) to dark brown when the grass looks rotten and is probably dead. The patches, which sometimes go paler with age, may extend until adjacent patches coalesce. When the disease is rampant, faintly pinkish white mycelium may be seen round the perimeter of the light brown patches. The disease can kill off a great deal of grass and severely damage a lawn. It may attack almost any turf but it occurs more frequently, and causes more damage, on intensively-managed fine turf which contains a good deal of annual meadow-grass and the worst attacks usually happen in the autumn on turf which has received nitrogenous fertiliser too late in the season. Prevention being better than cure, it is therefore wise to avoid giving late nitrogen (for example, after the end of August). The disease needs surface moisture, so switching or brushing the turf to remove water droplets from the grass-leaves during disease-encouraging weather is a help; so also is removal of any barriers to free air movement, which helps to dry out the surface. This may necessitate some attention to flower beds! Excessive amounts of top dressing, whether over the whole lawn or only parts of it, also encourage disease attack by smothering the grass and holding moisture on it. Sometimes an incipient disease attack can be halted by a change in the weather, for example, a change to dry or cold conditions, and a touch of ground frost at night has ended many a fusarium attack. Preventive applications of fungicide are not normally recommended for lawns but if the disease occurs and the weather conditions favour it then early application of fungicide is necessary, especially on fine lawns, to ensure that unacceptable damage is not caused. Indeed in severe attacks repeated applications may be necessary. There are various types of proprietary lawn fungicides available for use against fusarium disease. They are usually produced for application with added water by means of a suitable sprayer (Fig. 28) or with a watering can, preferably fitted with a dribble bar (Fig. 29). The maker's recommendations should be strictly adhered to and thorough safety precautions observed regarding toxicity hazards.

Corticium disease

Corticium disease (caused by *Corticium fuciforme*) seems to be becoming a more common problem on amenity turf than it used to be. In the past the disease seems to have had little more than nuisance value in the summer (particularly in relatively dry

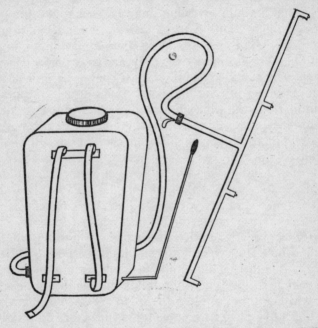

Figure 28 Knapsack sprayer for applying fungicide or selective weedkiller.

weather with dewy nights) but nowadays it is sometimes more serious and seems to attack throughout the year.

On domestic lawns it can be said, however, that the situation is pretty much as it has always been. During the summer patches of grass may take on a bleached but brownish look and, under close observation, small pink or red branched needles of the fungus may be found on the grass blades and sheaths. Fine fescues are usually the worst attacked but other grasses, including perennial ryegrass, may also suffer. Under lawn conditions the disease is seldom serious and may not need special treatment. For a summer attack a light dressing of nitrogenous fertiliser to cause the grass to grow away from the disease often

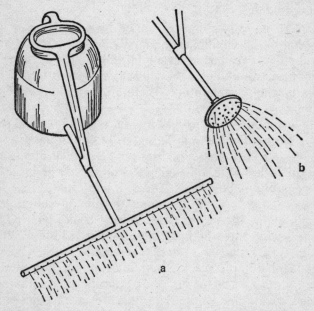

Figure 29   Watering can fitted with: (*a*) dribble bar, (*b*) fine rose.

proves very beneficial. In serious cases a suitable turf fungicide should be applied with due care.

Other fungal problems

Surface basidiomycetes. A fungal trouble which seems to have become more prevalent in recent years and which has not yet acquired a common name is caused by superficial Basidiomycetes which attack surface fibrous material in which they can be seen as white mycelium. There are believed to be several fungi concerned, one being *Cristella confinis*, but the others are as yet unidentified. They cause depressions in the surface, especially on fine lawns with a fairly thick fibrous layer, by

71

reducing the thickness in the patches attacked. The fungi seem difficult to control but, if control measures are desired, it is probably worth while giving the patches repeated applications of organic mercury fungicide—with due attention to safety precautions.

Fairy rings. Fairy rings are caused by soil-inhabiting fungi belonging to the Basidiomycete family which, starting from a central point, spread out in ever-widening circles, the mycelium of the fungus ramifying in the soil and, in the worst cases, more or less making it waterproof. There are several types of fairy ring.

The worst one (so called Grade 1 fairy ring) is caused by the fungus *Marasmius oreades*. This usually appears as two dark green rings with a brown or bare zone between; they may be quite small (less than a dinner plate) or very large indeed and stretching over whole fields. The soil, impregnated to a depth of 100–300 mm (4–12 in) or more with white mycelium, smells strongly of mushrooms and the fruiting bodies which appear on the surface are, in fact, tan-coloured toadstools. In the laboratory the fungus is readily susceptible to a number of fungicides but in practice it is very difficult indeed to eliminate, possibly because the fungus gains protection from the waterproofing effect it has on the soil which prevents fungicides from penetrating sufficiently. Because these fairy rings are so difficult to get rid of most people decide to tolerate them. The alternative is to dig out and take away all the affected turf and earth to a width of 300 mm (1 ft) clear of the green rings inside and outside the rings and to a depth of, say, 300 mm (1 ft) and then preferably sterilise the bottom and sides of the hole with formalin before replacing the excavated material with clean soil and new turf. Before embarking on such a vast undertaking it is prudent to consult an expert.

Grade 2 fairy rings show up as dark green ribbons or rings of grass on which puff balls or mushrooms may occasionally be found. One of several different types of fungus may be responsible and though they may dry out the soil there is no brown or dead area and the dense white fungal mycelium does not go as deeply into the soil as it does with Grade 1 rings. Once again people usually tolerate these since their effect is so small. In some cases they can be controlled by application (after spiking) of organic mercury fungicide well watered-in and this will usually at least prevent the production of fruiting bodies.

Grade 3 fairy rings are also produced by many types of fungus. There is no apparent effect on the grass but rings or groups of toadstools may appear. Control is probably unnecessary since the toadstools can be swept off or mown off but local application of organic mercury fungicide will usually stop the trouble if required.

NOTE: All fungicides are likely to be toxic and adequate safety precautions should be taken if, in fact, it is decided to use them on the lawn at all.

Pests

Birds

Starlings, rooks, jackdaws and other birds pay attention to turf mainly when there are grubs or insects of some kind in it. They may therefore serve as a warning that action is needed to deal with the infestation and, once the cause of their interest is removed, they soon go away.

Animals

Cats and dogs. On many lawns the chief pests are the neighbourhood's ill-trained cats and dogs, particularly the latter, and there are severe limits as to what can be done to stop their attentions. Once one dog or cat has used the lawn or garden as a lavatory it may well soon become a 'public' lavatory for dogs or cats and continue so for a very long time. Surface excreta should be removed, despite the unpleasantness of the task, and very often it is a good idea to give a copious application of water. Bitches do most damage in that their urine may cause severe scorch which is not seen until it is too late to do much about it. If it is seen in time thorough watering minimises the damage.

Field mice. Occasionally small holes made by field mice can be found and many people prefer to take no action since the field mouse seems to be regarded with some affection. Proud owners of very fine lawns, however, may have other ideas and try to get rid of them by trapping or gassing. Sometimes filling the holes and making life uncomfortable for the little animals succeeds in driving them away.

Moles. Lawns in urban areas are seldom disturbed by moles but elsewhere moles may invade from nearby land, where they are outside the lawn owner's control. Moles feed on earthworms for which they have a pressing and voracious appetite so that probably the best way of discouraging moles and their activity in producing mole hills, which can more or less destroy a good lawn, is to kill off the worms. Poisoning moles with baits is dangerous and trapping is best carried out by a professional mole-trapper if one can be found. In any case little permanent success can be achieved if the nearby land is full of moles! On large lawn areas, small paddocks and such like, effective control can be achieved through gassing the creatures with motor car exhaust fumes or through the use of special dusts which release toxic gases when moistened, these being blown into the runs by a special kind of blower or gas pump obtainable from horticultural suppliers.

Rabbits. Rarely a pest of domestic lawns, these animals can do a surprising amount of harm if they do occur. Their droppings are most noticeable and seem to foul the land. It is interesting to note that rabbits are selective grazers. On turf trial-grounds it has been noted that with various types of grass sward to select from, they show distinct preferences which vary from time to time without a very consistent pattern. They certainly favour succulent grass on newly-sown areas. Where rabbits are a problem, trapping them or wire fencing them out seem to be the most appropriate measures.

Rats. These occasionally cause damage to lawns which are near concentrations of the creatures in farm buildings or river banks. There are special baits obtainable from chemists which can be effective although they must be used with very great care. In some cases gassing as for moles proves a better approach. Trapping is seldom practicable.

Earthworms

The most common 'natural' pest is the earthworm. There are many species of earthworm but only two of these produce casts of earth on the surface of turf. In the garden as a whole, worms do a good job of work in mixing and aerating the soil, but worm casts on the surface of a lawn are unsightly and produce a muddy surface in wet weather, being especially a nuisance when the grass has to be mown. They also provide good seed beds for weeds and the presence of worms may lead to invasion by moles. Therefore most (though perhaps not all) lawn owners prefer a worm-free lawn.

Correct management can do a great deal to minimise earthworm trouble but control measures are sometimes necessary. If a wormy patch appears on a lawn it may be wise to apply a suitable wormkiller at an early stage and before the worms have multiplied and spread throughout the lawn. Worms are most active in warm, moist weather during late spring and early autumn. In cold, frosty weather and in dry weather they burrow more deeply into the soil. Worm-control treatments should, therefore, be given in the spring or autumn (preferably the latter) when the worms are near the surface and likely to encounter the control material before it is decomposed or dispersed.

Mowrah meal, a fairly safe product which used to be popular, brings the worms to the surface alive, but is difficult to obtain and is seldom used these days. Another product of vegetable origin, derris powder, is available and this is also fairly safe (except to fish) when applied as recommended. The rate of application for these products depends on the strength of the material obtained and it is usually best to water-in. Most of the worms are killed below ground but some come to the surface and need to be swept up. Control typically lasts about a year. Lead arsenate powder for which watering-in is optional, applied at 70 g per m² (2 oz per sq yd) kills the worms below ground and commonly gives control for at least five years but it is toxic and not easily available even to professional users. Chlordane products also give long-lasting control and are available in granular form for dry application or in liquid form for dilution in water and spreading with a watering can. The latter is preferred since it is more efficient and gets the bulk of the very poisonous chemical straight into the soil where it kills the worms but not the neighbour's pets. Carbaryl products are attractive because of their low toxicity (except to fish) but unfortunately their effects may be quite short lived. In use the proprietary carbaryl product, spread at the maker's recommended rate, is watered-in immediately after application. Most of the worms die in the soil but some come to the surface and these should be swept up and disposed of.

Because of their toxicity all wormkillers should be stored and used with great care according to maker's recommendations. If concentrated liquids come into contact with the skin the affected areas should be washed *at once*. Dry materials should not be spread without gloves and care should be taken not to breathe in dust or spray.

It is perhaps worth noting a further material which, though not as efficient as the other materials mentioned, is of little risk to turf, animals or humans. This material is, however, decidedly messy to use. It is potassium permanganate (obtainable from some chemists' shops) of which 17 g of crystals is dissolved in 5·4 litres of water for watering on to each sq metre (½ oz of crystals in 1 gal of water per sq yd). The permanganate is difficult to dissolve and stains everything it comes into contact with but, if applied during suitable weather when the worms are active, it does bring them to the surface. They are, however, not killed and so must be swept up!

Insect pests
There are quite a few lawn troubles which might arise from the activities of insects but fortunately they are not very common.

Ants. These do not often damage the turf but they sometimes produce small mounds of sandy earth and can be something of a nuisance. Ordinary soil insecticides are usually effective and so also are the special proprietary ant-killer preparations which are available.

Leather-jackets. The best known of the problems caused by insects is probably leather-jacket damage. Leather-jackets are the grubs of the daddy-long-legs or cranefly of which there are several species, the most common being *Tipula paludosa*. The grubs develop from eggs laid in late summer and feed on grass roots. When hatched a grub is very minute but as it feeds voraciously on plant roots it achieves a full size of 25–40 mm (1–1½ in) before turning into a pupa or chrysalis in the early spring. The grub is very tough, has no legs and its head is not very distinct. The presence of leather-jackets may be revealed only in late spring when the grass yellows or dies during dry weather and when they have pupated so that it is too late to take effective action against them, or by the activities of the birds which may come down for a feed. Damage caused by leather-jackets occurs mainly on weak turf in sandy (usually sea-side) areas. If the problem can be identified in time for control treatment to be worth while suitable materials include chlordane (as for earthworms), Gamma HCH and other proprietary soil insecticides. When damage is discovered, repair work may be necessary, by sowing seed or turfing as appropriate.

Miscellaneous insect pests. Occasionally, but rarely, other insect larvae or beetles can cause problems. These include mining bees, fever flies, St. Marks flies, chafers, cockchafers, Dor beetles, dung beetles and cut worms. Control measures are somewhat uncertain but treatment with soil insecticide may be worth while.

Weeds

Invasion and prevention
Weeds are said to be merely plants growing in the wrong place and, for the keen lawn owner, anything which is not good grass is

a weed. On the other hand there *are* people who don't worry about a very mixed herbage in their patches of lawn—and if this is liked or accepted by them why should they?

A lawn can often be kept clear of weeds for a very long time by good management. Regular mowing to a high standard with the boxing-off of cuttings is particularly important and so is using only just sufficient fertiliser of the right kind. Spreading weed seeds or runners in materials which are spread on the lawn, e.g. unsterilised compost, should be avoided.

Weeds reach the lawn in a variety of ways. Seeds or small pieces of viable runners may be blown on by the wind or carried on by birds. They may also be carried on footwear and on mowing and other equipment. If there is a dense unbroken turf cover, weeds have difficulty in getting established but any, even very small, patches of bare earth make it easier for them. General thinness caused by soil poverty, patches scalped by the mower, bare or weakened areas resulting from disease—all these help weed invasion. So also do the activities of casting earthworms which may bring weed seeds up from below the surface and, as well as smothering some of the grass, their casts provide a seed bed for these seeds and for seeds coming in from elsewhere. Anything which weakens the grass may let in weeds. Moss, which nobody seems to like in a lawn, is favoured by various 'grass-weakeners' including over-acidity, poverty and bad drainage. Strangely enough drought also leads to moss; a sward severely weakened by a long spell of hot, dry weather often becomes invaded by moss when the rains come. Of considerable significance in moss encouragement is shade, not only from trees and bushes, but also from overhanging flowering plants in the borders.

Control of broad-leaved weeds

The term broad-leaved weed is popularly used to include all common weeds of turf except weed grasses and the mosses. Before discussing chemical weed control it must be emphasised that hand weeding is never out of date. If the odd weed or small weed patch is dug out by hand that is the end of it; it doesn't have time to spread and the surrounding grass is not affected.

The grass *is* affected to some extent by weedkillers, even those that are selective.

For controlling miscellaneous weeds in a lawn, old-fashioned 'lawn sands' containing sulphate of ammonia and sulphate of iron mixed with sand and which achieve their results by preferential burning are seldom used for general weedkilling these days. Much better materials for this purpose are now readily available.

There are numerous proprietary products known as selective weedkillers which, used correctly, will eliminate weeds without killing the grass although its growth may be checked. Indeed it is sometimes a good plan to treat a weedy lawn with selective weedkiller just before going on holiday so that on return the weeds are gone and the grass is by no means as long as it would otherwise have been. The 'selective weedkillers' when absorbed by susceptible plants cause severe physiological disturbances resulting in ultimate destruction. Very often the first effect seen is the way the weeds seem to 'sit-up'—leaves of daisies, dandelions, etc., assume a rather twisted and more vertical position very soon after treatment but may take anything from several days to two or three weeks before finally dying.

The active ingredients in selective weedkillers are quite complicated chemicals with rather long chemical names but possessing also shorter and more commonly-used names: 2,4-D, MCPA, mecoprop, dichlorprop, fenoprop, dicamba, ioxynil. The proprietary lawn weedkillers contain one or more of these ingredients and it usually pays to buy a product containing more than one chemical because it is likely to cope with a wider range of weeds than a product with only one chemical. Before buying any particular brand find out whether it will kill all the different kinds of weeds which have been identified in the lawn. Some weeds such as plantains are killed by almost any selective weedkiller while others like the clovers are more difficult to get rid of. If all the weeds are not killed out by one treatment at the correct rate then another should be applied about a month later using the same weedkiller at the same strength or, if it is found that the weeds remaining are resistant to the product which has been used, then treat this time with a weedkiller to which they are susceptible. Mosses seem to be little affected by any of the selective weedkillers of the types under discussion—they are certainly not killed.

Selective weedkillers are supplied as concentrated liquids which have to be diluted with water before application. Professional turf managers usually apply them by means of a sprayer. This is the most efficient way of killing the weeds and may be a suitable procedure for very large lawn areas. For the average lawn owner, however, spraying involves too much risk of damaging drift reaching adjacent flower beds, etc., and so the weedkiller is applied in rather more diluted form and with larger droplets which do not readily become windborne, by means of a watering can fitted with a fine rose or with a dribble bar (see Fig. 29). For large lawns there is another possible approach—the use of a roller-type applicator which feeds the diluted weedkiller from a tank mounted on the frame so as to wet a special type of roller which in turn wets the foliage as it is passed over the surface of the turf.

Uniform application is important so as to avoid missing strips and thus leaving weeds, and to avoid excessive application through overlapping since this would damage the turf. Grasses are fully resistant only when the rate of application does not exceed maker's recommendations. It is worth while practising with plain water before making up the final weedkilling solution exactly as instructed by the maker. If there are only one or two weeds in the lawn it may, of course, be more appropriate to dig them out by hand. To avoid affecting the lawn as a whole, spot treatment of single weeds or weed patches may be undertaken by applying selective weedkiller by means of a sprayer or watering can, by using one of the aerosol packs now obtainable, or by rubbing with one of the small, solid, waxy preparations obtainable from some garden centres. It is, however, difficult to avoid overdoses and consequent damage to the grass on individually-treated patches.

Selective weedkillers may be applied at any time from spring to early autumn but the most satisfactory results are usually obtained in late spring. The best conditions are represented by fine, warm weather when the soil is moist and growth is vigorous. If it is windy, it is likely that weedkiller in spray or vapour form will get blown on to adjacent areas and rain falling shortly after application washes the weedkiller straight into the soil, so reducing its effectiveness very considerably. Treatment during drought or during the winter is not recommended since poor control of weeds is likely to be achieved and the turf may be damaged. After treating a lawn with selective weedkiller the turf should not be mown for two or three days or results may prove disappointing since much of the weedkiller will be removed before it has had time to be transmitted down to the roots.

Vigorous growth of the turf seems to help weedkill and certainly helps grass to fill in as the weeds die out. It is therefore often advantageous to apply a dressing of nitrogenous fertiliser one or two weeks before treating with weedkiller. There are combined fertiliser and weedkiller products on the market which, though probably not representing as efficient a procedure as just described, are very attractive to many lawn owners because of their convenience.

Selective weedkillers are very potent and affect other plants as well as weeds. Careless use, e.g. using a sprayer on a windy day, involves considerable risk to plants in flower beds and vegetable garden—not forgetting those in the neighbour's garden! If valued plants are believed to have been contaminated they should be well washed down with generous amounts of water in an attempt to save them. After use, equipment should be very thoroughly and repeatedly cleansed with water, and there are decided advantages in having a special watering can for weedkiller. For a week or two after selective-weedkiller treatment grass cuttings should not be spread directly among garden plants. They may be used for compost making but the compost should not be used for at least six months.

As with all chemicals used in the garden, weedkillers should be treated with respect. They should be stored with care, in a place where children cannot get at them.

Moss

There are over 600 different mosses in Britain although only a few occur in lawns. The average lawn owner lumps them all together as moss and, for reasons unknown, moss seems to be the most hated lawn weed. It is important to distinguish between moss, which is completely resistant to ordinary selective weedkillers, and the low-growing narrow-leaved weed, pearlwort, which is often confused with it since, although it is not one of the most susceptible of weeds, pearlwort *can* be controlled with selective weedkillers.

Mosses do not produce seeds but distribute themselves by various other methods, one of which involves the production of small spores in a structure known as a capsule which can fairly easily be seen at some times of the year. The spores are dispersed by the wind and when they germinate they produce a thread-like structure—protonema—which looks like a green algal growth. At this stage the moss is very susceptible to drought and so moss most readily invades areas where there is, at least at some time, plentiful moisture. Moss can also be spread through fragments of the plant becoming detached and establishing as new plants.

There are three types of moss commonly found in turf: trailing, upright and cushion moss. The trailing types are usually delicate fern-like mosses which may colonise extensive areas. Common examples are *Hypnum cupressiforme* and *Eurhynchium praelongum*. Upright types include *Polytrichum juniperum* which has fairly tall, stiff leaves that are dark green at the top but may be brown lower down the stem. Typical examples of the cushion type are the *Bryum* spp. These have small, upright and unbranched stems growing very closely together to form a dark green cushion which is usually soft to the touch. Mossiness is encouraged by several factors acting alone or in combination. They include low fertility, high acidity, excessive surface wetness, cutting too closely and poor light. On many lawns the edges become mossy because they are shaded by quite low-growing flowering plants which have been planted too near the edge of the lawn and so restrict the light and maintain a moist surface on the part affected.

To eliminate moss it is necessary to establish the causal factors and correct them as appropriate. Good moss killers are available but unless the causes are removed the moss will return.

There are various proprietary moss killers on the market. Many of them are based on calcined sulphate of iron which has a burning-out effect which is comparatively short lived and/or calomel (mercurous chloride) which is slow acting but long lasting.

The old-fashioned, but still useful, lawn sand consisting of sulphate of ammonia, sulphate of iron and sand in the right proportions may not be much used for general weed control but, applied in the growing season (preferably in the spring), it often gives good control of moss as well as stimulating the grass. Proprietary lawn sands of this type vary in their composition but a good mixture is three parts sulphate of ammonia and one part calcined sulphate of iron mixed with ten parts medium sand and this is used at 136 g per m² (4 oz per sq yd). Best results against moss are obtained from these products if they are applied on a dewy morning with a dry, sunny day to follow. The soil should be moist. If no rain falls within forty-eight hours watering-in is necessary to prevent too much burning of the grass. A week or two later scorched moss should be gently raked out and collected with a wire rake. The turf, stimulated by the sulphate of ammonia, should soon recover from an initial scorching, become dark green and start growing into the areas vacated by moss. Repeated treatments are sometimes necessary.

Products based on calomel alone are very slow to act and may show little benefit for many months. Calomel does, however, prevent spore formation and it is used advantageously with sulphate of ammonia and sulphate of iron plus a carrier of sand to produce proprietary mercurised lawn sands for spring and summer use or, in admixture with sulphate of iron and carrier plus little or no nitrogenous fertiliser, for autumn and winter use. It is not advisable for the lawn owner to attempt to produce home-made mixtures of these chemicals because of the toxicity risk and indeed this type of moss killer is sometimes difficult for the amateur to obtain.

Some other materials are available commercially for treating moss. Dichlorophen and chloroxuron are two new moss-killing chemicals which are quite effective and which are available in proprietary products but which may prove rather expensive. Indeed all the good moss killers tend to be costly and this emphasises the value of sound management to keep out the moss. Moreover, direct moss control is likely to prove of only short-term value if the causes of the moss are not dealt with.

When using moss killers it is, as always, important that maker's recommendations are adhered to and care taken to avoid damage caused by excessive application. This advice is of particular significance when treatment is confined to affected areas of turf only and very often it is wise to treat the whole lawn in a uniform manner.

Lichens

Lichens are primitive plants occurring commonly on walls, rocks and tree trunks but occasionally they occur in lawns, with their sometimes over-lapping leaf structure taking on plate-like form. Usually lichens appear on turf which is very weak because of wetness or over-acidity. The best method of control is to ensure vigorous grass growth by removing the cause of its weakness. In some cases a dressing of the lawn-sand-type moss killer in due season is worth while.

Algae

Bare ground in a lawn, particularly in wet, shaded areas, sometimes becomes covered with a slippery scum of algae which may vary in colour between green, blue-green and even black. If surface moisture can be got away by aeration and the grass can be persuaded to grow into these areas this soon ousts the algae, but its disappearance can be helped by watering on sulphate of iron solution at the rate of 50 g in 8 litres water to 4 m² (1½ oz in 1½ gal to 4 sq yd) or by using a dichlorophen-type moss killer.

Weed grasses

Whereas many people are satisfied if their lawn is covered with grass of any kind, most people regard some grasses as weeds. Indeed, some of the grasses which are deliberately sown for the coarser type of lawn are regarded as weeds in a fine lawn.

The two most common weed-grass enemies are, however, the

natural invaders Yorkshire fog (*Holcus lanatus*) and annual meadow-grass (*Poa annua*). Yorkshire fog appears in unsightly coarse patches in all types of lawn but annual meadow-grass while starting with odd plants or patches, usually spreads rapidly to mix completely with the existing grasses and even to supersede them in course of time. Many fine lawns contain a very large proportion of annual meadow-grass so that if it were possible to eliminate it by means of one treatment with a suitable chemical there would not be much grass left!

To date there are no chemicals which can be recommended for selective killing of weed grasses in turf. Correct management can help considerably to keep out and restrict the spread of annual meadow-grass but is seldom entirely successful. Yorkshire fog patches, if not too plentiful, can be replaced by good turf. The alternative is regular severe scarification of individual patches of Yorkshire fog (possibly with an old kitchen knife or even the half-moon edging iron). Sustained treatment of this kind will at least disguise the blemishes and may even be successful in eliminating the Yorkshire fog and encouraging its gradual replacement by other grasses.

Miscellaneous problems

Abandoned lawn

When moving into a new house it is possible to find that the lawn has been neglected for quite a long time and it may look as though it is beyond redemption. Indeed if there is a great deal of coarse grass and many weeds, or a great thickness of fibrous material at the base of the grass, it may well be best to dig up and start again. On the other hand, if there is a predominance of acceptable grass and not too many weeds it may be worth while restoring the existing turf, especially since the new householder has so many calls on time and money.

The first step is to remove any stones or debris from the lawn and then cut down the grass *in stages* over a period of a week or two by the most appropriate means. This may involve anything from a pair of hand shears to a large rotary mower (possibly hired). A dressing of complete fertiliser is probably advisable as the grass reaches the required shortness which can be mown with the ordinary mower and, as it regains its natural colour and vigour, some scarification may be required. Problems with mat or thatch, weeds, pests, compaction, etc., can then be dealt with as appropriate with due attention to season and to weather conditions.

Banks

Banks tend to make mowing difficult. This is especially so if they are too steep or if the upper edge is not gently rounded or flattened and the bottom gently tapered out to the general level below. Banks may need at least as much attention as the rest of the lawn in respect of aeration, feeding and watering.

Bare patches

The first step is to find the cause and take appropriate action. If a bare patch results from excess of a persistent type of chemical in the soil it may be necessary to replace this soil. If there is a topsoil deficiency, this should be corrected. The best approach to actual renovation depends on the season as well as what is reasonably convenient. Re-turfing can be carried out at almost any time of the year provided the new turf can be kept moist in dry weather but is best done in autumn. Re-seeding is best done in spring or very early autumn but may be successful in summer.

To re-turf a relatively small patch, a good plan is to obtain a suitable square of turf, lay it over the bald patch, and cut the old turf vertically to the appropriate depth using the edges of the new turf as a guide. When the old turf is then taken away the new turf should be an exact fit and can be laid neatly on the soil. The soil below should of course be loosened slightly and the holes adjusted to the right depth to receive the new turf at exactly the right level. The new turf should not be above the general level of the lawn. A little top dressing rubbed in, especially at the edges, finishes off the job. To obtain a suitable square of turf in the first place it may be possible to take a piece from a good but unimportant area of lawn and replace it with the bad material.

If a bare area is to be re-seeded it is necessary to prepare a reasonably satisfactory seed bed without too much disturbance of the earth below. A suitable procedure might be to give the area a good pricking with a garden fork and scratch up a shallow seed bed of loose soil with a garden rake or even with a small hand fork before sowing seed (to match the lawn) at about 35 g per m² (1 oz per sq yd). The seed should be gently raked in or covered with a very thin layer of screened topsoil or compost before being pressed down gently, for example with a board. It may be desirable to protect from birds by using a few strands of cotton on short sticks or even to cover the patch with poly-thene for a *few* days (until the grass is through) so as to keep off the birds and to hasten germination.

Bents

In mid-summer irritating wiry stalks are sometimes seen sticking up here and there after the lawn has been mown. These are commonly referred to as *bents*. They are generally flowering stems, usually of perennial ryegrass but sometimes of other grasses such as fine bent grass. They do not appear very often under a regime of regular and efficient mowing and sufficient scarification but, once they show up, it seems necessary to cut them off individually by the most convenient means.

Brown patches

A common question from worried lawn owners is 'What causes the brown patches on my lawn and what can I do about them?' Usually a straight, simple answer cannot be given because the brown patches may result from a variety of causes including:

(i) Scorch by chemicals (including fertiliser).
(ii) Scorch from animal urine.
(iii) Drought.
(iv) Disease (there are several possibilities here).
(v) Pest damage.
(vi) Spilt oil or petrol.

The appropriate remedy clearly depends on the cause. The immediate answer to the first three problems and even the last may be to give plenty of water, while for Nos. (iv) and (v) the right treatment can be decided only when the cause has been identified. Spillage of oil or petrol can be avoided by oiling and refuelling the mower somewhere other than on the lawn.

Daffodils and mushrooms

Many people are attracted by the idea of using the lawn area to grow bulbs or mushrooms. Unfortunately the idea does not work out very well mainly because of mowing requirements. Allowing the grass to grow long weakens and thins the turf so it is not recommended. On the other hand, mowing off the foliage of the bulbs soon eliminates these. If bulbs are to be grown then some sacrifice of lawn quality is necessary. However, by planting the bulbs in not too plentiful clusters or drifts, the areas of lawn which are marred can be minimised.

Mushrooms don't have much chance to appear in regularly-mown turf and in any case mushrooms are usually difficult to establish in a lawn. If they do grow, they may be responsible for one type of fairy ring.

Lawn edges

Regular attention to lawn edges ensures that they will be smart. However, unless there is permanent edging support, in the course of time and with regular work on adjacent flower beds the edges become broken and uneven. They may be trimmed with a half-moon tool or with a *straight*-bladed spade but if this is done too often the lawn steadily shrinks. Sometimes it pays to cut a 300 mm (12 in) square of turf which includes a broken edge, to push it out until the broken part overhangs the adjacent area and then trim off straight with the rest of the lawn edge (Fig. 30). The space behind can be levelled up with soil and either seeded or turfed. If preferred the square of turf cut out may be turned round so that the broken bit is within the lawn where seeding can be carried out after the levels have been made good with topsoil. Another possibility is to exchange the whole of the square with a sound piece from within the lawn.

Where lawn edges have no permanent support, repeated trimming with a spade or half-moon edging iron will tend to make the lawn smaller gradually. To reverse the situation it is often a good plan to lift a 300 mm (12 in) width of turf round the edge and re-lay to the correct position. The space behind it is then made up with topsoil before sowing matching grass seed.

Mat or thatch
Many old-established lawns, particularly fine lawns, develop a surface layer of fibrous material which may be 25–150 mm (1–6 in) deep. This may be mainly above the soil when it is described as thatch or to some extent integrated with the surface soil when it is usually termed mat (see Fig. 2) but the difference between the two terms is not always distinguished. The

Figure 30 Repairing a broken edge.

layer of fibrous material is formed from a variable mixture of dead plant material in various stages of decay together with living (possibly moribund) stems and roots. It lies below the green aerial growth and restricts moisture penetration so that a fibrous turf is likely to have poor drought resistance (the soil below remaining dry) and poor disease resistance (moisture being retained at the surface). There are believed to be several factors which may contribute to the formation of this excess fibre, including especially bad drainage and over-acidity. Where a mat of excess fibre exists it is therefore worth considering whether either of these needs attention.

To reduce the amount of fibre, severe scarification with a wire rake or, better still, with appropriate mechanical equipment is necessary. This may need to be repeated at appropriate seasons over a period of years. Only comparatively light scarification with a mechanical scarifier is usually acceptable during the spring and summer because of possible disfigurement and the fact that the treated turf becomes more susceptible to drought. Early autumn is the best time to make a big effort to reduce the fibre since at this season really dry conditions are unlikely to reoccur and there is still growth to assist recovery if any damage is done.

In extreme cases it may be worth considering lifting and re-laying the lawn. This involves cutting the turf as thinly as it will lift (leaving most of the fibre behind) and placing it aside so as to allow the remaining fibre to be carried away or dug in and a good turf bed prepared before re-laying the turf. Professional help and equipment is likely to be needed for this operation!

Poor surface levels

A lawn with a bumpy surface is difficult to mow properly, especially at low heights of cut. Minor unevenness can be rectified over a period by regular top dressing but marked bumps and hollows need more severe action. Repeated hollow-tine forking of a bump will in time take out sufficient earth to lower it as the surrounding earth will slowly settle into the holes. A hollow can be raised by the following procedure. First use a half moon (or spade) to make a series of parallel vertical cuts about 150 mm (6 in) deep and 100–150 mm (4–6 in) apart. Then with a garden fork prise up successive strips of turf between the cuts and put earth down the crevices formed so that when the turf is released the level of the hollow is raised to that of a straight-edge placed across it (see Fig. 31).

It is sometimes necessary to have a more radical approach and to lift the area of affected turf plus a little margin, adjust the levels by adding or taking away topsoil and then to relay the turf. If topsoil is removed care must be taken to ensure that 100–150 mm (4–6 in) is left under the turf—if necessary some subsoil may have to be removed to ensure a reasonable depth of topsoil for the turf. For small areas it may not be necessary to remove the turf completely—it may be sufficient to just roll it back while level improvement is taking place.

Scalping

Mowing the grass too short where there is an uneven surface leads to the mower scraping off the tops of the high places—scalping. The remedy is to mow less closely until the surface has been made sufficiently smooth.

Shade

If lawn grass does not grow very well because it is shaded by buildings or by valued trees and if a lawn is still wanted, then the best plan is to let the grass (of whatever kind) grow rather longer and to mow it only at a height of 50 to 75 mm (2 to 3 in). In extreme cases it may be necessary to re-seed or re-turf

Figure 31   One way of raising a hollow.

annually. Wood meadow-grass which some people believe to be suitable for shady lawns does not like cutting at all and does not survive even the longest normal cutting heights.

Shortage of root

Shortage of roots leads to an unthrifty turf with poor drought resistance. There are several possible causes including soil compaction and bad drainage. Aeration of some kind helps a lot, particularly hollow-tine aeration in the autumn. A few months after this operation has been carried out cutting out a turf will reveal groups of new white roots down the holes.

Thin and sparse turf

The possible causes are numerous. They include over-acidity, shortage of mineral nutrients (poverty), poor aeration, drought, bad drainage. It is usually necessary to identify the cause (or causes) and take corrective action. After this it may be worth while oversowing the thin area or even the whole lawn with suitable grass seed in due season after scarifying well. The seed should then be covered lightly with top dressing.

Trees

Despite their obvious attractions, beautiful trees and good lawns are uneasy companions. Trees which are anywhere near a lawn are liable to make the lawn short of water, short of plant foods, short of light and to pollute it with leaf drop, whilst autumn leaves, unless swept up promptly, can smother the grass and encourage disease. Seeds of ash and sycamore establish beautifully in hollow-tine holes! Judicious pruning of branches or roots is sometimes of considerable assistance to the lawn.

Washboarding

Lawns sometimes develop a regular unevenness in the form of waves or ripples in more or less straight lines reminiscent of the old-fashioned washboard. This effect is believed to be caused by regular mowing in the same up and down direction. The undulations affect the actual soil and are considered to be related to a regular pattern of vibration from the mower. Changing the direction of mowing each time the grass is cut prevents this fault from occurring. Where the trouble has already developed top dressing will smooth out the surface.

Wear

There is a limit to the amount of wear that turf will endure. This is particularly true of fine turf required to be in first-class condition so such turf should not be abused. On the other hand, the delicate creation which receives no wear at all can be very difficult to maintain especially as it will readily produce an excessive layer of soft fibre mat or thatch; *some* wear is of assistance in producing a good turf but it is unwise to have narrow connecting stretches which attract excessive use.

Lawns which are much used by children should preferably be of the medium type rather than the fine type since this kind of sward is more robust. Good drainage in the broadest sense makes a very important contribution to durability since wetness makes the turf more easily damaged and extra forking may be required. A little extra fertiliser over the growing season helps to keep the grass in constant recovery from wear but excess of fertiliser is likely to lead to soft, easily-damaged growth.

When wear results in thin and bare areas then renovation with seed or turf in due season becomes necessary.

Wetness

Bad drainage does not seem a very common problem on domestic lawns but difficulties do occasionally arise. A wet, muddy lawn results when surface water can not get away sufficiently quickly. This may be due to the soil draining poorly because of its heavy nature or because of compaction. In either case aeration in due season, particularly hollow-tine aeration, will help considerably. If the wetness problem remains it may prove necessary to do something about subsoil drainage. Sometimes it is sufficient to install a sump at the lowest corner of the lawn (see Drainage).

Worn out lawn

Occasionally a new house owner finds a lawn which has been so neglected that the grass has more or less disappeared, having been superseded by moss and weeds, possibly with some bare ground. In some cases the situation may be dramatically changed over a period of a few months by liming (if soil tests show over-acidity) and generous fertiliser treatment. Such treatment often reveals that there is more grass (and fine grass at that) present than was apparent at first and treatment can then be continued by giving more fertiliser and then weedkiller (or fertiliser/weedkiller combined). However, waiting for results that may not be obtained can waste a lot of time so that a decision to make a new lawn is usually the right one. The existing herbage may be dug in or, sometimes, scraped off to rot down into organic compost for the vegetable or flower garden. If the existing turf is to be dug in it may be worth while spraying it beforehand with a short-lived total herbicide such as a product containing paraquat and diquat (remembering, of course, that these chemicals are dangerous poisons).

5

Maintenance Equipment

There are quite a number of items of equipment used in lawn maintenance. Some are used regularly, some very rarely and, of course, some have a dual function, being used for the garden in general as well as for the lawn. Few lawn owners will possess or need *all* the equipment listed below. Usually people acquire many of the items in course of time as need arises or opportunity offers. It is well to remember that in total they represent a considerable investment and therefore reasonable storage facilities are most desirable. Mowers stood outside with only a plastic sheet over them or with no cover at all are unlikely to provide good service for very long.

The most important and almost the only essential item is clearly the mower and it is wise to buy the best suitable mower that can be afforded. It should be well looked after with cleaning and oiling or greasing every time it is used. At the end of the main mowing season it should be thoroughly gone over and if necessary sharpening and repair work arranged to be done during the winter.

Possibly the next most important requirement is to have something with which to trim the lawn edges. Hand shears will do but long-handled shears are better. They should be rubbed dry after use and then wiped with an oily rag, especially at the end of the season. There are, of course, various mechanical lawn-edge trimmers for those with a lot of edging or who are gadget minded.

A spring-tined wire rake is very useful indeed, its main use being to scarify the surface of the lawn but it is also useful for collecting fallen leaves.

Many lawn owners like to keep their lawns green and pleasant looking in dry weather and so, particularly for those in dry areas or those who have a very sandy soil, some arrangements for watering are needed. A hose-pipe with a fine rose may be convenient on very small areas but a good sprinkler represents a considerable advance. It allows an even spread of water to be applied in a gentle rain over a period while the owner does other jobs. Care should be taken to see that there are no leaks from the sprinkler itself or from its connection with the hose-pipe which would cause detrimental ponding on the lawn.

Brushing up leaves, scattering worm casts and dispersing dew can be accomplished fairly comfortably with a stiff broom. A besom is slightly better in some cases, and for large lawns it is worth while having a switch for dispersing dew and scattering worm casts. On large lawns surrounded by trees it may be worth acquiring a purpose-made leaf sweeper.

Aeration of a kind can be accomplished with a garden fork but there are special hand forks available for both solid- and hollow-tine aeration. For larger lawns there are small machines for this work and some of these machines have alternative fittings for scarification. It should be noted that some of the cheap equipment sold for lawn use may not be very effective.

If top dressing is 'home-made' then a simple lightweight sieve with 6 mm (¼ in) mesh may be needed to prepare the material for application, but it is becoming more common for those who do bother to top dress to buy ready-prepared material. Whatever bulky top dressing is applied a shovel is required for spreading and the material has to be worked into the surface with a view to smoothing this out. A rake (such as a wooden hayrake) which possesses a flat back is often sufficient, but keen types may wish to buy a metal drag mat, a drag brush or a lute.

A watering can with a fine rose for application of weedkillers, wormkillers or fungicides is necessary on occasion. A special fitting known as a dribble bar is a great help in getting a good coverage without using too much water. For large lawns a special lawn sprayer may be worth while but if this is used for weedkilling there is always some risk of drift harming adjacent flower beds, even if the edges are done separately with the watering can.

Spreading of fertiliser (powdered materials being the most favoured) is usually best done by hand with the exercise of a good deal of care. However, many people prefer to buy or hire a small distributor, a piece of equipment which might well give false confidence. It can be difficult to match up adjacent breadths and turning at the ends creates problems which are best overcome by doing the turning outside the lawn area.

For obtaining a neat edge to a lawn that has no permanent

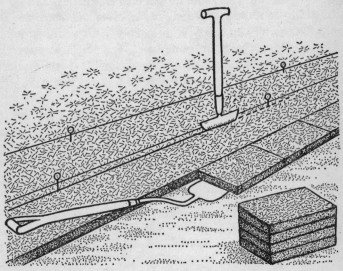

Figure 32   Using a half-moon edging iron and a turf float.

edging and for cutting out patches during repair work, a half-moon edging iron is extremely convenient. A turf float for lifting turf (e.g. when doing repairs) is likely to prove an unnecessary luxury (Fig. 32).

There is no need for edging with a half moon if permanent edging is set just below the turf surface. Wood and concrete are very good for edging but are quite expensive and are laborious to install, whereas special metal edging, though not so permanent, can be bought cheaply and is easy to position—the work may be completed in about an hour on a typical small suburban lawn.

Useful ancillary items include a garden line (for edging) and a straight plank 2–4 m × 150 mm × 38 mm (6–12 ft × 6 in × 1½ in) for edging and for helping in level regulation whether by top dressing or by turf adjustment. An old kitchen knife or something similar is handy for severe scarification of small patches of Yorkshire fog.

6

Lawn Calendar

It is impracticable to manage a lawn to a precisely-timed programme and the timetable given here is for general guidance
only. Variations in soil, climate, locality, weather and so on,
have a considerable bearing on what things should be done and
when, so that intelligent interpretation is necessary. *Not* everything listed needs to be done; a lawn needs *regular* attention but
it does *not* involve a life sentence of hard labour.

January

This is often the worst month of the year weather-wise and the
lawn should be more or less left alone and not trodden on,
particularly if it is waterlogged or affected by frost. It should,
however, be kept under observation for possible disease attack;
any in-blown leaves should be cleared and not allowed to
smother patches of the turf.

Supporting work may be done of course, e.g. mower repairs
and top dressing preparation. Any uncompleted turfing should
be finished if the right conditions occur.

February

Also a bad month for weather, February sometimes provides
milder periods towards the end of the month, particularly in the
south of England. These may encourage earthworm activity and
if casts become numerous they should be swept off when the
surface is dry. However, it may be too early for successful
wormkilling since many worms are likely to remain deep in the
soil out of harm's way.

If the weather is particularly mild, brushing or light scarification may be worth while and a winter-type moss killer may be

applied if considered necessary. Mild weather may bring disease especially in sheltered corners.

March

March usually brings the first signs of spring weather and appreciable growth is likely to be seen so that the first mowing becomes necessary. There is no need to rush into this and it is sometimes beneficial, before mowing starts, to roll the lawn lightly to firm up the surface which may have been affected by winter weather conditions. In the absence of a very light garden roller sufficient rolling might well be accomplished by using the mower (if of suitable type) with the cutting part held clear. Before rolling, a thorough brushing and/or light raking with the wire rake is usually needed to disperse worm casts and gather up twigs and other debris which the wind has blown on to the grass.

When the grass has straightened up after rolling it should be cut with the blades set high—only light topping is required at this stage. Mowing should be done when the surface is dry and during mild weather since cold winds are likely to discolour and check the new-mown grass. Only one or, at most, two cuts should be needed in March.

Wormkiller may be applied if necessary at a time when the creatures are working near the surface. Inspection for disease is particularly important in March and April.

Unsupported lawn edges sometimes get damaged when work on the borders is being done and this is a good time to trim them with a half-moon edging iron using a straight-edge or tight string as a guide where appropriate.

April

Spring weather is now really starting and increased growth calls for more mowing although the height of cut should be lowered only gradually and the summer cutting height reached only by the end of the month at the earliest; early May is usually soon enough.

Top dressing may be done this month and the second half of the month is a good time to apply spring fertiliser where required. This can be followed up after seven to fourteen days with selective weedkiller if necessary. Instead of ordinary fertiliser mossy lawns can be treated with spring and summer moss killer. Whether or not fertiliser is used, good growth should obtain when selective weedkiller is applied if good results are to be assured. When there are only a few weeds hand weeding or spot weeding may be better than treating the whole lawn with weedkiller and coarse grass plants can be eliminated only by hand weeding.

Any bare or thin patches should be renovated with seed.

May

This is often a dry month but there is usually sufficient moisture in the soil to ensure good growth and the summer routine of regular mowing at the required height should gradually become established. Watering may sometimes be beneficial. Selective weedkilling may be done if necessary.

In May and June annual meadow-grass seeds profusely and is very conspicuous on fine lawns. Drag brushing or light raking before mowing brings the panicles up to a level where the mower can remove them.

June

The peak season for mowing is now coming and the mowing routine should be strictly adhered to but if a long, dry spell occurs it may be wise to raise the cutter and even to remove the grass-box (and thrower plate where appropriate). Edges should be trimmed every time the lawn is cut. Regular light scarification is appropriate with particular attention to any clover runners. Selective weedkiller may be applied where needed.

July

This is a month for regular mowing and regular light scarification, the latter more particularly on fine lawns. Edge trimming should not be forgotten and watering may be necessary in dry weather. Selective weedkilling is still possible and it is often a good plan to apply weedkiller before going on holiday, especially if a substitute mower operator is not available! It is wise in any case to hold off mowing for a few days after weedkiller application to allow the weedkiller to be absorbed and the check given to grass growth reduces the amount of grass to be tackled on the holiday-maker's return. It is, however, recommended that alternative arrangements should always be made for mowing during holiday absences.

August
Lawn treatments should generally be as for July but a final dressing of nitrogenous fertiliser may be given towards the end of the month to help maintain sufficient growth during the autumn months. This is really the last good month for weedkilling since, apart from reduced efficiency of weed control, as the autumn approaches there is less vigour in the turf to fill up spaces left by departing weeds.

September
As the month passes growth falls off a little and it may be possible to reduce mowing frequency. At the end of the month the height of cut should be raised a little.

This is a good month to carry out severe scarification where there is an excessive layer of mat or thatch. Any patches which become very thin as a result of the treatment and bare patches resulting from wear or any other cause can be sown over with matching grass seed. Lawn repair by turfing can also be done towards the end of the month as well as during October.

Regular inspection for disease should be maintained so that, in the event of an attack, fungicidal application may be made before the turf is appreciably damaged.

Late September is a good time for aeration and top dressing.

October
There is less mowing to do now and the cutting cylinder should be set to the winter height to help the grass have sufficient strength to withstand winter weather. Mowing should nevertheless continue whenever the growth exceeds this height appreciably. A better job of mowing is accomplished when the lawn is dry and very often if a rain-free day occurs dry conditions may be helped along by brushing off dew and rain drops an hour or two before mowing.

Aeration and top dressing should be completed this month. There is often a regular chore of sweeping up leaves which would otherwise weaken the turf and lead to disease attack. Inspection for disease is important this month, particularly in mild, moist weather. Wormkilling should be carried out if necessary.

Trimming the lawn edges may see them through the winter.

This is a good month for doing any re-turfing work necessary.

November

Mowing with the cutter set relatively high may be required on one or two occasions only but care is needed to choose the right days when the surface is dry and firm and there is no frost about. Wormkilling may still be possible if mild weather encourages the worms to work near the surface. Equipment should now be cleaned up, oiled, etc. The leaf problem usually persists.

December

There is little to do with the lawn itself but sweeping up leaves may still be necessary, keeping off the lawn in very wet or frosty weather as much as possible. Where there is proved over-acidity in the soil this is a suitable month to give corrective lime treatment. If, despite adequate aeration, the lawn is wet and soggy plans should be made to install suitable drainage as soon as opportunity offers.

Glossary

Ameliorant: Something to improve or make better. The most commonly used materials for physical amelioration of the soil are sand and peat.

Biodegradable: Biodegradable materials are decomposed by bacteria, etc., and so do not persist in the soil.

Compost: Material for lawn top dressing and typically resembling a sandy loam enriched with organic matter. 'Real' compost is prepared by building up a heap from alternate layers of soil and rotted farmyard manure (or other organic matter), allowing to stand a year, then breaking down and mixing with sand. Substitute composts may be made by mixing up soil, sand and peat or other suitable organic material for immediate use.

Cultivar: *Culti*vated *var*iety of a turfgrass species.

Drag brush: A drag brush is pulled along to smooth out top dressings and work them into the sole of the turf. It has a specially-shaped head with long, stiff bristles. A drag brush may also be used to give gentle scarification, to disperse dew and to scatter worm casts.

Drag mat: A flexible steel mat with uses similar to those of a drag brush. For working in top dressings on a surface where undulations are appropriate a drag mat is preferred to a drag brush which is more suitable for dead-level surfaces.

Fallowing: Leaving untilled and unsown for a time. In practice, fallowing implies leaving the land without grass or any other crop for a short period until weeds develop, removing these by cultivation (or chemical treatment) and repeating the whole procedure for, preferably, a whole summer season.

Friable: Crumbly, easily crumbled.

Grading: Adjustment of site gradients, regulating levels.

Leaching: Washing out of salts by water percolating through the soil.

Loam: A useful intermediate type of soil—without too much sand or too much clay.

Lute (or loot): A lute is a tool for smoothing out loose surface material and a simple version can be produced from a piece of wood 915 mm (3 ft) long by 75 mm (3 in) wide and 20 mm ($\frac{3}{4}$ in) thick fixed to a handle so as to somewhat resemble a garden rake. More sophisticated versions can be purchased.

Mat: A layer of fibrous vegetation at the base of the green grass foliage and partly married with the surface soil. It is sometimes fairly loose and soft but often quite tight and firm.

Microbiological: Pertaining to minute living organisms especially bacteria and fungi.

Mulch: A loose surface cover of suitable material spread to reduce moisture loss by evaporation.

Mycelium: The mass of white threads arising from the spores of a fungus. Mycelium threads are often grouped together to appear almost solid.

Nap: When the grass foliage all lies in one direction there is said to be a nap (compare a billiard cloth).

Panicle: Loose, irregular type of compound inflorescence such as the flowering head of grasses.

Procumbent: Prostrate, growing along the ground.

Recumbent: Lying down.

Rhizome: An underground creeping stem (usually white or brown). Smooth-stalked meadow-grass is rhizomatous.

Soil structure: In a natural soil the various ultimate particles (sand, silt, clay) are grouped together and the term *soil structure* refers to the manner in which these particles are assembled or arranged. In a normal soil the particles are grouped together into aggregates and the size and shape of these aggregates and the distribution of channels between them has a considerable bearing on the properties of the soil. For turf the aim is to encourage and maintain a good crumb structure in which the crumbs are water-stable aggregates, possibly the size of small peas. Structure can be destroyed by working wet soil but grass roots promote crumb formation.

Soil texture: Refers to the proportions of the different sized particles in the soil, i.e. to the proportions of sand, silt and clay.

Spp.: Abbreviation for species in the plural.

Stolon: Creeping stem above ground level, usually green, rooting at the nodes (joints) and there giving rise to vegetative shoots and stems. Lawns are sometimes produced from the stolons of creeping bentgrass.

Sward: An area covered with short grass—hence also the actual covering, i.e. the turf.

Thatch: A layer of fibrous vegetation at the base of the green grass foliage which is typically fairly loose and soft and not integrated with the surface soil.

Tillering: The formation of side-shoots from the base of the grass plant. (See Fig. 33.)

Tine: A spike. Aerating equipment is fitted either with solid or hollow tines. (See p. 60 and Fig. 26.)

Top dressing: The application of suitable bulky material to the turf. The main purpose is surface improvement. Also refers to the material used.

Unthrifty: Not thriving.

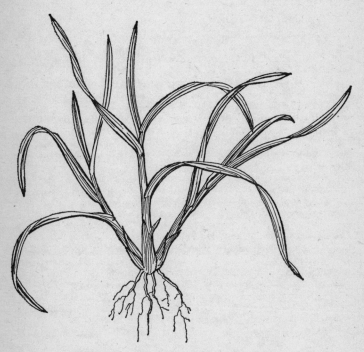

Figure 33   Typical grass plant showing tillers.

Further Reading

ABC of Turf Culture, J. R. Escritt, Kaye & Ward, 1978. A text-book on turf in encyclopaedia form.

Chemical Weed Control in Your Garden. A very useful thirteen-page booklet produced by the Agricultural Research Council Weed Research Organisation, Ed. J. E. Y. Hardcastle, Revised 1978. It deals with flower beds, etc., as well as lawns.

Dawson's Practical Lawncraft, R. B. Dawson and R. Hawthorn, Crosby Lockwood Staples Ltd., 7th edn., 1977

Directory of Garden Chemicals, British Agrochemicals Association, 3rd edn., 1978. A list of garden chemicals with the names of their suppliers and some hints on sensible usage.

Fungal Diseases of Turf Grasses, J. Drew Smith and Noel Jackson, Sports Turf Research Institute. An authoritative text-book on turf diseases with useful colour illustrations. Out of print but possibly available from libraries.

Grasses, C. E. Hubbard, Pelican, 1968. A detailed book on grass identification, etc.

How Grasses Grow, R. H. M. Langer, Edward Arnold Studies in Biology No. 34, 1972. Quite a simple book but possibly a little technical for some.

Soils and Fertilisers (Horticultural Science and Soils, Vol. 2), E. G. Coker, Macdonald Horticultural Series. Easy-to-read information on soil matters including moisture characteristics, biology, etc., and also on mineral nutrients needed for plant growth. Out of print but possibly available from libraries.

The Wild Flowers of Britain and Northern Europe, R. Fitter, A. Fitter and M. Blamey, W. Collins Sons & Co. Ltd., 3rd edn., 1978. A beautifully-illustrated book which should help in weed identification.

The World of the Soil, Sir E. John Russell, Fontana (New Naturalist), 1974. A very readable text-book on soil.

Metric/Imperial Equivalents

TEMPERATURE

°F	°C
45	7
50	10
55	13
60	16
65	18
70	21

LENGTH

in	cm
$\frac{1}{4}$	0·6
$\frac{1}{2}$	1·3
1	2·5
12	30
24	60

WEIGHT

oz/sq yd	g/m²	oz	g
1	35	1	28
2	70	4	113
3	100	16 (1 lb)	454
4	140	36 ($2\frac{1}{4}$ lb)	1000 (1 kg)

AREA

1 sq yd = 0·8 m²
$1\frac{1}{4}$ sq yd = 1·0 m²

VOLUME

pints	litres
$\frac{1}{2}$	0·3
1	0·6
$1\frac{3}{4}$	1·0

Note: These conversions are approximations.

Index

turf 1–5, 98, *see also* new
   lawn
   edging 33
   re-turfing small areas 86,
      101, 102
   thin and sparse 91–92

unthrifty turf 8, 104

washboarding 92
water 63–67, 100
   alternative to 67
   amount 64
   application of 64–65
watering can 95
wear of lawn 92–93

weed grasses 1, 49, 84–85
weedkillers 32–33, 79–81, 93,
   100–101
weeds 39, 86
   broad-leaved, control 78–
      81
   invasion and prevention
      77–78
wetness 93
wetting agents 65
wire rake, spring tined 94
wood meadow-grass 25, 91
worn out lawn 93

Yorkshire fog 3, 85, 97

THE BASICS OF GARDENING

ALAN GEMMELL

Do you know why roses are pruned? Do you know how to diagnose iron deficiency, what the effects of mulching are, how a compost heap works, why fruit trees are grafted onto rootstocks?

The Basics of Gardening will answer all these questions by giving you the principles behind common gardening practice. With this background knowledge of soil, climate and plant science you will be able to find solutions to problems in your own garden whether these are concerned with protected cultivation, pests and diseases, the use of fertilizers and manures or hydroponics.

Alan Gemmell retired from the Chair of Biology at Keele University in 1977 and for 31 years has been a regular panellist on the popular BBC radio programme, Gardeners' Question Time.

TEACH YOURSELF BOOKS

POPULAR AND EXOTIC HOUSE PLANTS

ERIC ROBERTS

Growing indoor plants is not only a very satisfying hobby but also a particularly beautiful form of home decoration.

This book provides all the information necessary for growing a wide range of indoor plants. Initial chapters cover general topics such as watering, feeding, potting, propagation, pests and diseases and these are followed by a comprehensive A to Z of house plants, both popular and exotic.

Detailed instructions are given on the care of individual varieties and the plants are graded according to the degree of attention they need.

TEACH YOURSELF BOOKS

GROWING VEGETABLES

TONY BIGGS

Everything you could want to know about vegetables from planning your vegetable garden, soils and plant nutrition, principles of crop rotation to crop harvesting and storage, and a summary of what to do when round the year.

This is a book for all gardeners whether you have a walled kitchen garden or only a windowsill, patio or roof-garden. The beginner will find the basic approach particularly helpful but there is also a wealth of useful information for the experienced gardener.

Tony Biggs is Lecturer in Horticulture, Wye College, University of London where his speciality is vegetable crops. Besides lecturing and researching on the subject he is also a keen gardener and his family are self-sufficient in vegetables.

TEACH YOURSELF BOOKS